OUTRAGE

OUTRAGE

How Gay Activists and Liberal Judges Are
Trashing Democracy to Redefine Marriage

PETER SPRIGG

Since 1947
REGNERY
PUBLISHING, INC.
An Eagle Publishing Company • Washington, DC

Library of Congress Cataloging-in-Publication Data
Sprigg, Peter.
 Outrage : how gay activists and liberal judges are trashing democracy to
redefine marriage / Peter Sprigg.
   p. cm.
 ISBN 0-89526-021-2
 1. Same-sex marriage—United States. I. Title.
 HQ1034.U5S67 2004
 306.84'8'0973—dc22
                      2004012849

Published in the United States by
Regnery Publishing, Inc.
An Eagle Publishing Company
One Massachusetts Avenue, NW
Washington, DC 20001
Visit us at www.regnery.com

Distributed to the trade by
National Book Network
4720-A Boston Way
Lanham, MD 20706

Printed on acid-free paper
Manufactured in the United States of America

10 9 8 7 6 5 4 3 2 1

Books are available in quantity for promotional or premium use. Write to
Director of Special Sales, Regnery Publishing, Inc., One Massachusetts
Avenue, NW, Washington, DC 20001, for information on discounts and
terms, or call (202) 216-0600.

CONTENTS

INTRODUCTION

BY TONY PERKINS
PRESIDENT, THE FAMILY RESEARCH COUNCIL

As a former legislator, I spent considerable time developing and debating public policy. There was a reason I was involved in public policy and there continues to be a reason. Public policy is critical in a democratic republic like ours. Public policy has the power to shape our culture. That is why the founders assigned policy-making responsibilities to the elected branch of government closest to the people—the legislative branch.

If one doubts the power of public policy to shape our culture, consider the last radical social policy experiment on the family: no-fault divorce.

What has been the result of the policy of no-fault divorce? A 34 percent increase in divorce between 1970 and 1990. Some point out that divorce has declined in the last decade, which is true, but only because marriages have declined and cohabitation has risen nearly ten-fold. There has been a 141 percent increase in single-parent homes, leaving more children in poverty than there were in 1972. The public policy of no-fault divorce has had disastrous consequences for the family and has caused irrefutable damage to millions of children.

It is important to note that the same arguments used to advance no-fault divorce are being used again, this time to support same-sex marriage: "It will make marriage better," "It will be good for children."

No-fault divorce was a public policy initiative that has knocked the institution of marriage to its knees and weakened it to the point that homosexual radicals are now moving in for the kill—this extreme shift in public policy that would embrace same-sex marriage will be the end of marriage as we know it. Indeed, in the areas of Scandinavia where de facto gay marriage, by way of civil unions, has gained acceptance over the last decade, marriage itself has declined and is becoming the exception rather than the rule.

Is that what we want for America?

Outrage will assist the reader in understanding what is at stake in the public policy debate—the future well-being of our children and grandchildren.

PREFACE

To judge by public opinion polls, those of us opposed to homosexual marriage are winning the day. Very few Americans want our laws to be changed to allow homosexuals to "marry." Yet in terms of political action, the pro-family, pro-marriage majority has been strangely muted. And I believe the reason is that this silent majority feels ill-equipped to defend marriage (which they take for granted), and to refute the rhetoric of homosexual activists.

The purpose of this book is to fill that gap.

As I show in this book, the debate over "gay marriage" is the culmination of a thirty-year struggle by liberal activists to change the definition of marriage. That effort has failed completely at the ballot box, has made only small inroads in democratically elected legislatures, but has finally broken through in the courts—an ominous sign for democracy, as well as for marriage. In fact, many constituencies not usually associated with the "pro-family movement" have good reasons to oppose the push for same-sex marriage, including Democrats, libertarians, and even homosexuals themselves, as I'll show.

Homosexual activists' most effective argument is that same-sex marriage is a "civil rights" issue. They argue that they are being denied "equality" under the law. I'll show why they're wrong and why "sexual orientation" is a category utterly unlike race, and therefore unworthy of special protections. The "civil rights" argument is also undermined by the overwhelming opposition of African Americans to homosexual marriage, and I refute the specious analogy between bans on interracial marriage (which reinforced the unrelated practice of racial segregation) and bans on homosexual marriage (which go to the heart of what marriage and the family are).

Having thus disposed of red herrings and properly defined the issue, the heart of the book deals with the tangible reasons—rooted both in the nature of human beings and the findings of social science—for preferring marriage between one man and one woman and opposing any other definition. Emotional appeals claiming that homosexual couples want to marry for the same reason as heterosexual ones miss the point. The real question is why such private relationships should be treated as a public institution in the first place. The only justification for government involvement in marriage is to promote the family—a union of a man and a woman for begetting and raising children.

I'll also answer the question that homosexual activists consider their trump card—"What harm could it possibly do to someone else's marriage if a gay couple gets married?" In fact, we know what society's seal of approval would do: legitimize the infidelity and instability that characterize homosexual relationships and put more children into families in which they often suffer harm—as demonstrated in their own poignant words, some of which are quoted in this book. And finally, legalizing homosexual marriage would indeed put us on a "slippery slope" toward the legalization of marriages based on polygamy, incest, or even pedophilia.

One thing absent from the arguments thus far is religion. This disproves the notion that opposing homosexual marriage is a narrowly sectarian religious viewpoint or an arbitrary moral judgment. Even those who are utterly irreligious have abundant reason to oppose the push for homosexual marriage.

But having made the secular arguments, I do offer a principled defense of the right—the constitutional right—of religious people to bring their convictions to bear on issues of public policy. I also offer a brief theological explanation as to why the Bible and Christian tradition are clearly against homosexual marriage.

One question remains—what to do about it. In the final chapter, I explain where the threat to marriage is coming from—not just from the legislatures, but from the courts; and not just in the states, but at the federal level. I show why the threat of a U.S. Supreme Court ruling declaring same-sex marriage the law of the land is an imminent one—and why passage of a Federal Marriage Amendment is the only solution.

If you thought religious conviction was the only reason to oppose homosexual marriage—you'll think again after reading this book. If you thought no one could give a reason why homosexual marriage will hurt the family and the country—you'll think again after reading this book.

If you think homosexual marriage is something good for the country, irrelevant, or only vaguely unsettling—think again.

It's an outrage. And it's time to take action to stop it.

1

Who Declared This Culture War?

HOW WE GOT HERE

Among certain homosexual activists and segments of the liberal media, there is a standard line regarding how homosexual marriage became a hot political issue in 2003 and 2004. The argument is that President Bush is seeking to shore up his base of support among the so-called "religious right" in anticipation of his 2004 bid for reelection. Some say he wants to distract the public's attention from the "quagmire" in Iraq. Therefore, he has chosen to launch a new "culture war" against gay and lesbian Americans by announcing his support for a constitutional amendment that would "write discrimination into the Constitution" by banning gay marriage. In doing so, the president has taken actions that are "polarizing" and "divisive."

This was the line taken by Doug Ireland in the liberal magazine *The Nation*, under the headline "Republicans Relaunch the Antigay Culture Wars":

As George Bush's poll numbers began seriously dwindling, Karl Rove and the White House political strategists decided to reach into their bag of tricks and come up with a good old staple of reactionary politics: homophobia.[1]

A spokesman for the Gay and Lesbian Alliance Against Defamation used similar rhetoric, referring to Marriage Protection Week (for which President Bush had issued a proclamation) as "the antigay industry's latest effort to inflict discrimination on hapless gays and lesbians."[2]

Yet this is nonsense. When we have a fundamental institution of society such as marriage, whose basic definition as the union of a man and a woman has remained unchanged in Western civilization for millennia, surely the faction that seeks to merely retain what until now has been entirely taken for granted cannot be accused of being "divisive" or "polarizing." Quite apart from the merits of the argument, any remotely honest or objective observer would have to recognize that the people responsible for dividing society over the definition of marriage are those who want to change its fundamental definition, not those who want to preserve it.

Even some homosexuals themselves (particularly those who recognize that public opinion is strongly against homosexual marriage, and rightly fear a "backlash" against the campaign for it) have made exactly this point. Bruce Carroll, a former member of the gay organization known as the Log Cabin Republicans, declared this in the *Washington Blade*, a gay newspaper:

[I]t wasn't the "religious right" or President Bush who started this round of the culture war. It was us. The battle was clearly started by gay activists who adopted the tactic of challenging marriage laws across the country.[3]

Carroll is exactly right. It is not conservatives who have launched a "culture war" over homosexual marriage. Instead, it is homosexual activists themselves who have launched a sneak attack designed to bring the pillars of American culture—marriage and the family—toppling to the ground. And complicit in this attack are America's courts and their black-robed judges.

The Black Plague

Discussions of homosexual "marriage" among homosexuals themselves can be traced back at least fifty years. And, though it may surprise some, lawsuits demanding a right for homosexuals to "marry" date back over thirty years. A fact that is too little known is that numerous court cases (nearly two dozen, by one count)[4] dating back to 1971 have been decided in a way that completely rejected the arguments in favor of homosexual marriage, creating a large body of precedent on which today's courts could and (under the established legal principle of *stare decisis*: "stand by that which is decided") should rely. Far from being a rising tide, court decisions in *favor* of homosexual marriage represent only a trickle. But that trickle threatens to change American society forever.

Due to a series of early court decisions rejecting homosexual marriage, the idea was never really taken seriously until the early 1990s, when courts in both Alaska and Hawaii considered suits demanding a right to homosexual marriage. In the Hawaii court, a ruling was actually handed down saying that homosexual couples must be given the right to marry. However, in both Alaska and Hawaii (as in thirty-six other states since), the people rose up to take back control of their government from the courts by passing state constitutional amendments effectively overturning the pro–homosexual marriage decision. In Hawaii, the amendment merely declared that the legislature would have the power to define marriage as the union of a man and a woman—which it subsequently did. However, Hawaii also threw one bone to the homosexual activists by adopting a form of domestic partner benefits—albeit while creating a broader category of "reciprocal beneficiaries" that could include, for example, people related by blood who are ineligible to marry one another.

The homosexual marriage cases in Hawaii and Alaska not only galvanized the people of those states to rise up in defense of marriage, but also triggered a national response. Fearing that if even one state legalized homosexual marriages, those marriages might then have to be recognized in every state and by the federal government, pro-family forces got a bill introduced in Congress to accomplish two things. First, the bill declared that for every purpose under *federal* law (such as taxation, Social Security, immigration, and federal employee benefits), marriage would be defined only as the union of one man and one woman.

Secondly, the bill declared that no state would be *required* (although neither were they forbidden) to recognize a same-sex marriage or other same-sex union that was legally contracted in another state. Since marriages in one state are normally recognized by every other state, the concern was that the germ of homosexual marriage in one state might soon infect the entire country. Homosexual activists have argued that such recognition is required by the U.S. Constitution's "full faith and credit" clause, which reads, "Full Faith and Credit shall be given in each State to the public Act, Records, and judicial Proceedings of every other state." (Article IV, Section 1). However, in passing the Defense of Marriage Act (DOMA), Congress was acting pursuant to the power granted to it in the following sentence of that section, which declares that "Congress may by general Laws prescribe the Manner in which such Acts, Records, and Proceedings shall be proved, and the Effect thereof." Congress was also acting in accordance with a longstanding principle of interpretation regarding "full faith and credit" known as the "public policy exception," which allows states *not* to recognize acts of other states if to do so would violate a "strong public policy."

The Defense of Marriage Act passed both houses of Congress by large bipartisan majorities, with most Democrats joining almost all Republicans in support (a notable exception was Senator John Kerry). President Clinton signed the bill in 1996, declaring through a spokesman his opposition to homosexual marriage in the process.

Passage of the federal DOMA had its intended effect, leading many states to pass their own individual statewide DOMAs declaring that homosexual marriage was contrary to the "strong public policy" of that state. Each DOMA was different.

Some were passed by the legislature, some by referendum (like California's Proposition 22 in 2000). Language varied. Some were just statutes, while some were state constitutional amendments. But the passage of thirty-eight state DOMAs by 2004 showed a strong national consensus in favor of defining marriage as the union of one man and one woman.

Despite this evidence of an overwhelming consensus in favor of the historic and natural definition of marriage, homosexual activists continued to press their case in the courts. They knew that even a statutory DOMA would not prevail if a state's supreme court determined that it violated that state's constitution. And no state limitation on the definition of marriage would be able to withstand a ruling by the Supreme Court of the United States on federal constitutional grounds.

In Vermont, homosexual activists scored their first major success. In the case of *Baker v. State*, the state's supreme court ruled in late 1999 that homosexual couples must be offered the same legal benefits as married ones. With this gun to its head, the Vermont legislature created a parallel to marriage that it called "civil unions," rather than grant the full status of civil marriage to homosexual couples. Signed into law by Governor Howard Dean, "civil unions" became law in 2000.

Yet homosexuals continued to strike out in their efforts to win civil marriage, losing cases in the lower courts of Indiana, New Jersey, and Massachusetts. This continued to be the case even after homosexual marriage achieved its first legal foothold anywhere in the world, when the Netherlands became the first country to grant the full rights of civil marriage to same-sex couples in 2001. Belgium followed suit in 2003.

However, two events in the same month—June 2003—catapulted homosexual marriage from a cultural issue to a hot political issue in the United States.

Canadian Gay Marriage and *Lawrence v. Texas*

The first of these events was the decision of the highest court in the Canadian province of Ontario on June 10, 2003, ruling that the Canadian Charter of Rights and Freedoms requires that marriage be granted to homosexual couples. The ruling was handed down without a stay, so the first legal homosexual marriages in the Western hemisphere took place later that same afternoon in Toronto. A court in British Columbia soon followed suit, and the Canadian federal government, which had been undertaking a fairly thoughtful and considered study of the whole issue of homosexual marriage, basically threw in the towel and said it would introduce legislation to make homosexual marriage the law of the land throughout Canada (a proposal that has since stalled because of unexpectedly strong resistance to gay marriage even among our liberal northern neighbors).

Somehow, it was easy to ignore homosexual marriage when it was just a cultural experiment in the socialist countries of Europe. It became a much more immediate threat (or realistic hope, depending on your perspective) when it became a legal reality in our nearest geographic and cultural neighbor.

Then, only sixteen days later, came the U.S. Supreme Court's decision in the case of *Lawrence v. Texas*, in which the Court struck down a Texas law that made "homosexual conduct" a criminal offense, effectively declaring homosexual sodomy to be a constitutional right. In doing so, the Court took the extraordinarily rare step of explicitly overturning a precedent set only seventeen years before, when it had upheld a Georgia sodomy law in the case of *Bowers v. Hardwick*. A bare majority of five justices found in *Lawrence* that outlawing specific sexual acts between persons of the same sex violated the "right to privacy" that the Court has inferred (in cases like *Roe v. Wade*) from the Constitution's guarantee in the Fourteenth Amendment that no state shall "deprive any person of life, liberty, or property, without due process of law." Justice Sandra Day O'Connor concurred in the decision, but on other grounds, viewing the application of the law only to homosexuals (and not to people committing the same sexual acts with people of the opposite sex) as a violation not of the "right to privacy," but of the same constitutional section's guarantee of "equal protection of the laws." The remaining three justices—Scalia, Thomas, and Chief Justice Rehnquist—dissented.

The Texas law struck down in *Lawrence* differed from the Georgia law upheld in *Bowers* in one important respect. The Georgia law had been more sweeping in scope, prohibiting specific sexual acts whether committed between sexual partners of the same or opposite sexes. The Texas law was targeted only at homosexual conduct. Therefore, it would have been logically possible for the Court to strike down the Texas statute without overturning *Bowers*, simply by following the logic of Justice O'Connor in ruling on "equal protection" grounds. Under such an opinion, the logic would have been that declaring certain acts illegal when committed by sexual partners of the same sex, but tolerating the exact same acts when committed by partners of the opposite sex, violated this principle of equality.

Such a decision would have still allowed prosecutions for sodomy, as long as the law applied to both homosexual and heterosexual acts. But some observers felt that an "equal protection" ruling might actually carry a greater danger in the long run, because its rationale would be more directly applicable to marriage. If one argues that it violates the Constitution to treat sexual acts differently under the criminal laws merely on the basis of the sex of one's chosen sexual partner, then it would have been only a short step to argue that it is equally a violation of the "equal protection" principle to treat relationships differently under the marriage laws merely because of the sex of one's chosen life partner.

Thus, on the face of it, the *Lawrence* decision could be interpreted as containing a silver lining for the defense of natural marriage. After all, to say that a right to privacy prevents the state from punishing certain relationships as criminal is not to say that the state has an affirmative mandate to *reward* such relationships by granting them the privileges of marriage.

Nevertheless, it soon became apparent that any silver lining in *Lawrence* with respect to marriage was very thin indeed. Homosexual activists and the media immediately seized on the ruling's general effect in advancing the homosexual agenda for acceptance, and identified marriage as the next frontier to be conquered. And conservative doomsayers had no less an authority than Justice Antonin Scalia himself as support for the fear that *Lawrence* would lead directly down the path to homosexual marriage.

Justice Scalia reached this conclusion by noting that the Court had rejected the state of Texas's contention that moral disapproval of homosexual acts was in and of itself a sufficient basis for declaring such acts to be criminal. Scalia argued that if morality were to be disallowed as a "rational basis" for law, then many other longstanding laws would have to fall as well, given that they have little basis other than the protection of "public morals." He named as one example laws limiting marriage to a man and a woman. Scalia added that the Court, in its majority opinion, had done nothing to "cabin"—that is, limit and restrict—the effect of its decision from such a conclusion.

I believe Justice Scalia was wrong on two counts. First, it is simply not true that *nothing* was said by the justices in the majority that might "cabin" the decision from having an effect upon marriage. For example, Justice Kennedy said the ruling did not address "whether the government must give formal recognition" to homosexual relationships, and he distinguished the sodomy law from ones designed to prevent "abuse of an institution the law protects."[5]

Second, as I argue elsewhere in this book, it is not only a mistake but also a grave error to suggest that moral judgments are the *only* basis for limiting the definition of marriage. The definition of marriage as the union of one man and one woman is rooted in the immutable and empirical facts of nature with respect to human reproduction, quite apart from any subjective moral judgment.

However, having said that, there *was* much in the *Lawrence* decision that endangers traditional marriage. For one thing, the majority opinion of Justice Kennedy made it clear that the Court chose to rely on the "privacy" and "due process" arguments rather than "equal protection" in order to *broaden* the scope of the ruling, not to narrow it. Ironically, this broadening effect came about because of a narrowing of the ruling's focus. The *Bowers* decision was neutral in its application, criminalizing specific sexual acts whether committed in a homosexual or heterosexual context, though the Court's decision was based specifically on its unwillingness to declare *homosexual* sodomy to be a protected right.

In *Lawrence*, by way of contrast, the Court was presented with a law of which the unique feature was its targeting only of homosexual acts. But the Court's ruling did not limit itself to the issue of this narrower targeting of homosexual sodomy. Instead, in overruling *Bowers*, the Court issued a ruling that (by striking down *all* sodomy laws) created a sexual privacy right for everyone.

Kennedy's opinion did not suggest that sexual privacy was the real issue that the majority was concerned about. Instead, it appears that the real reason the Court struck down *all* sodomy laws was not out of concern for the sexual privacy of heterosexuals but to ensure that no *homosexuals* would ever be prosecuted for sodomy again, regardless of how inclusive the law might be. The *Bowers* and *Lawrence* decisions had this in common—their main impact was on the issue of sexual privacy, based on reasoning limited to homosexuality.

So in analysis, what the Court said about sodomy (or even about morality as a basis for law) is less important that what it said about homosexuals themselves. And here, there is certainly cause for concern. Justice Kennedy made many sweeping statements about the lives of homosexuals as a class that could certainly be applied to marriage. Indeed, one of the reasons cited for striking down the sodomy laws was because they could be used to justify "discrimination" in other areas of life. Given that the Supreme Court has never declared sexual orientation to be a protected class under civil rights laws, one might well wonder why this would even be a concern for the Court, unless it is deliberately driving a social agenda of its own preference.

In a narrow sense, the ruling in *Lawrence* should apply only to the criminal law, and have nothing whatsoever to do with marriage. However, the language of the decision itself betrayed the Court's unwillingness to construe the Constitution "in a narrow sense," and strongly suggested that the Court, as Justice Scalia explicitly charged, was taking its place in the culture war on the side of homosexuals. This does not bode well for marriage.

Goodridge v. Department of Public Health

The next event, which transformed homosexual marriage from a gathering storm to a raging hurricane, was the decision of the Massachusetts Supreme Judicial Court in the case of *Goodridge v. Department of Public Health*. In this case, seven homosexual couples filed a suit demanding the right to obtain marriage licenses. They were rebuffed in a lower court ruling when the judge told them that the issue was one they had to take to the legislature, not to the courts. Nevertheless, many observers expected that the highest court in Massachusetts, because of the state's liberal reputation, would be the first to rule in favor of civil marriage for homosexual couples.

Oral arguments in the case were held in the spring of 2003. Under the court's normal procedure (but not a binding rule), decisions are handed down within 120 days of oral argument. The deadline for the decision came in July 2003, within weeks of the Ontario ruling and the *Lawrence* decision. That deadline came and went.

Finally, on November 18, 2003, the court handed down its decision. By the narrowest of margins, 4–3, it ruled that under the Massachusetts Constitution's guarantee of equal protection, marriage could not be limited to opposite-sex couples. The court rightly rejected the contention that Massachusetts law already allowed homosexual marriages, ruling that both legislative intent and common-law traditional practice defined marriage as the union of a man and a woman. *But the court declared that it was unilaterally changing the "common" law to define marriage as the union of "two persons."* John Adams, the author of the Massachusetts Constitution, must have been rolling over in his grave.

The decision brought a simmering debate over proposals for a Massachusetts defense of marriage amendment straight to the front burner. In the previous legislature, an effort to place such an amendment on the ballot through an initiative petition process had failed through parliamentary chicanery. Under Massachusetts law, an initiative that has received the required number of signatures needs the support of only 25 percent of the legislature, meeting in joint session as a constitutional convention, to get on the ballot. However, when the convention met, the senate president immediately adjourned it without a vote, thus killing the amendment.

In the 2003–2004 session of the Massachusetts legislature, pro-family forces tried a different approach, introducing a constitutional amendment in the legislature itself. The new amendment was called the Marriage Affirmation and Protection Amendment, or "MA & PA" for short. A scheduled meeting of the legislature to consider the amendment in November had been postponed pending the *Goodridge* decision, but after the ruling came down, all eyes became focused on the new date for the convention in February. Some politicians in the state, ever eager to find ways to vote both sides of an issue, sought an opinion from the Massachusetts Supreme Judicial Court (known as the SJC) as to whether civil unions like those adopted in Vermont would satisfy the ruling of the court. The answer seemed obvious from the court's original November ruling, but just to emphasize it, the SJC issued an advisory opinion in February saying no, only civil marriage would do.

What appeared, however, to be a clear-cut choice—between an amendment to protect marriage or an endorsement of the *Goodridge* decision—proved to be anything but clear-cut in practice. An apparently unlimited ability to offer substitute amendments on the floor of the constitutional convention in place of the one originally filed in the legislature led to intricate parliamentary maneuvering, several continuations of the convention, and eventually a back-room deal among the legislative leadership that led to passage of a revised amendment that declared marriage to be between one man and one woman, but that at the same time created civil unions within the constitution.

The amendment process in Massachusetts requires that the same amendment be approved by a majority of the next legislature (that is, not before 2005), after which it would be placed on the ballot at the next general election (November 2006), where it would need majority approval of the voters in order to become part of the constitution.

The problem is, the court in the *Goodridge* decision stayed its order for only 180 days, or until May 17, 2004—not long enough for the amendment process to be completed. In fact, it remains entirely unclear at this writing what will become of the legal same-sex marriages in Massachusetts when the voters render them illegal (or at least, not civil marriages) by amending the constitution in 2006. Additional legal moves failed to block the *Goodridge* decision before the May 17 deadline, so Massachusetts had the first legal same-sex marriages in the United States.

Law professor Lino Graglia has exposed the real agenda behind these developments—the destruction of democracy. Graglia agrees that we are in a culture war, but explains that it not simply between liberal and conservative:

> It is a war between our cultural elite... on the one hand, and the ordinary American citizen on the other. The average citizen holds views on a wide range of issues of basic social policy... that are anathema to our cultural elite. The difficulty with our system of representative self-government, as the intelligentsia sees it, is that everyone gets to vote, with the result that the views of the unenlightened masses are likely to prevail.
>
> The function of constitutional law, in the view of our cultural elite and as it has largely operated in recent decades, is to keep this from happening.... [J]udges, given a free hand in policymaking, can generally be relied on to serve as the mirror, mouthpiece, and enacting arm of liberal academia in general and liberal legal academia in particular.

Graglia explains how this phenomenon plays out with respect to homosexuality:

> Decisions extending marital rights to homosexual unions do so on no other basis or authority than the fact that full societal acceptance, if not endorsement, of homosexuality is the current cause célèbre in today's academia. The primary function of judicial opinions explaining these decisions is to deny or conceal this fact and to perpetuate the fraudulent claim that they are the commands of pre-existing law.[6]

Mayor Newsom and the Illegal Licenses

Mayor Gavin Newsom of San Francisco, the unofficial capital of "gay" America, apparently decided that Massachusetts judges shouldn't get all the credit for having the first government-sanctioned homosexual marriages. So, on February 12, 2004, he announced that he would issue marriage licenses to homosexual couples and have city officials "marry" them at City Hall. This led thousands of homosexual couples (including Rosie O'Donnell and partner) to stream to San Francisco in the subsequent weeks in a quest for that coveted "license." It also led to a spate of copycats, as local officials in New Paltz, New York, in New Mexico, and in Oregon all followed suit in issuing marriage licenses to homosexual couples.

There was only one problem with all these homosexual "marriages." Every one of them was completely illegal. A couple filling out a government marriage license does not make the couple legally married, even if a public official performs the wedding. Defining who is eligible for marriage is a function of state law, not local practice, and no local official can change the law of an entire state.

It might be one thing if an official tried this stunt in a state where marriage has never been defined by statute (a state like, say, Massachusetts). California, however, is not such a state. Instead, California has a Defense of Marriage Act, adopted by 61 percent of the voters in a referendum in 2000, that clearly defines marriage as the union of a man and a woman. Newsom maintains that he was acting in obedience to a higher law, the California Constitution, which guarantees the "equal protection" of all its citizens (sound familiar?). But if rewriting the constitution to make it say something its actual authors never intended or even could have conceived of is outrageous when done by four judges, it is even more so when decided unilaterally by a single local official.

Fortunately, all of the renegade homosexual marriages were eventually shut down by legal action in the various states that witnessed them. In fact, some officials, such as the mayor of New Paltz, New York, were actually charged with criminal offenses for knowingly solemnizing an illegal marriage. Some of the cases have now resulted in the initiation of new *Goodridge*-like lawsuits seeking a court declaration of the right to homosexual marriage.

It's clear that homosexual activism brought us this debate. But what are the primary arguments involved? We'll begin to examine that in the next chapter.

2

Why Libertarians (and Other People Who Might Surprise You) Should Support the Federal Marriage Amendment

The debate over homosexual "marriage" is one fraught with stereotypes. I'm not talking about the stereotypes of homosexuals. Instead, I'm talking about the stereotypes of the people opposed to homosexual civil marriage. To judge by the language of homosexual activists, their postmodern liberal allies, and their friends in the media, there is only one type of person who could possibly have any motivation for opposing giving the full rights of civil marriage to homosexual couples. Such a person, according to this stereotype, would have to be an ignorant, right-wing, Christian fundamentalist.

But given that 72 percent of the American public opposes homosexual civil marriage,[1] it's obvious that a lot of people who favor the natural definition of marriage don't fit the stereotype.

One of the battlegrounds for homosexual marriage is Massachusetts. The governor, Mitt Romney, a moderate Republican, is opposed to legalizing same-sex marriage. So is the heavily Democratic legislature, which has even voted in favor of a state constitutional amendment to define marriage as a union of one man and one woman (though it would allow civil unions for homosexuals).[2] Massachusetts is one of the most liberal states in the union, but the majority of its people oppose same-sex marriage.

Yet in Massachusetts, established law and the will of the elected governor, the elected legislature, and of the people themselves has been overturned by the renegade judges of the Massachusetts Supreme Judicial Court, who voted 4–3 to assert that the Massachusetts Constitution requires that homosexual couples be allowed to marry. In February 2004, the court went even further. It declared that "civil unions" short of marriage would not do.

On May 17, 2004, Massachusetts witnessed the first legal homosexual civil marriages. It was a historic day. It was also an outrage to the Massachusetts Constitution and to government of the people, by the people, and for the people. It was an act of judicial tyranny at the behest of an activist minority group.

Despite the broad support for the historic definition of marriage throughout the population, some groups have been seduced by the homosexual movement into accepting, or at least into not resisting, the calls for homosexual marriage. One example is "libertarians"—those who place individual liberties above all other political or social values. Their opposition to government's imposition of moral standards on private behavior has led some libertarians to support same-sex marriage. But such a view reflects a misunderstanding of what's at stake in the political battle over this issue.

So, rather than devote this chapter to the arguments against homosexual marriage that one might expect to hear—based on religion, history, and tradition—I want to begin with an argument that might be counterintuitive and show why libertarians (and some other people who might surprise you) should oppose homosexual civil marriage.

Homosexual Marriage Is Not a Privacy Issue

Perhaps the most common "libertarian" argument in favor of the homosexual activist position on homosexual marriage is the notion that the government should not interfere with people's private lives or judge their private sexual behavior, as long as it takes place between consenting adults. Privacy from government intrusion is one of the key values of a libertarian worldview.

But there is one big problem with using the "privacy" argument: *Respect for the "privacy" of homosexuals is an argument for abolishing sodomy laws—not an argument for recognizing homosexual "marriage."* And that is a battle that homosexual activists have already won. In its landmark ruling on June 26, 2003, the U.S. Supreme Court, in the case of *Lawrence v. Texas*, struck down sodomy laws as an unconstitutional violation of the "right to privacy," which the Court inferred from the "due process" clause of the Constitution.[3]

That inference is hard to justify on strict constitutional grounds, yet there is no political movement to amend the Constitution to overturn the *Lawrence* decision. Indeed, if homosexual activists had been willing to stop there—with legal "toleration" of their sexual behavior—there would not be much political debate about homosexuality today.

But the push for homosexual marriage is different because it is *not* a privacy issue. Demanding that the government officially and legally recognize homosexual relationships as civil marriages is a public issue and *invites* government "interference" in their relationships. Friendship is a private matter. Sodomy is now officially a private matter. *But marriage is a public institution.*

A libertarian believes that people should be free to enter (and leave) personal relationships at will. And where legal implications are unavoidable (as in the ownership of property), the parties can arrange their affairs using private contractual arrangements. The key point is that homosexual couples can arrange their affairs freely *right now, under current law.*

Taken to its logical extreme, this privatized view of marriage could lead to its abolition as a distinct legal structure. Yet what homosexual activists currently seek is not such freedom from government interference, but the *expansion* of state-sanctioned marriage to include homosexual couples.

Homosexuals Seek to Turn Marriage into Another Government Entitlement Program

One of the key arguments often heard in support of homosexual civil marriage revolves around all the government "benefits" that homosexuals claim they are denied. Many of these "benefits" involve one thing—taxpayer money that homosexuals are eager to get their hands on. For example, one of the goals of homosexual activists is to take part in the biggest government entitlement program of all—Social Security. Homosexuals want their partners to be eligible for Social Security survivors' benefits when one partner dies.

The fact that Social Security survivors' benefits were intended to help stay-at-home mothers who did not have retirement benefits has not kept homosexuals from demanding them. Nor did it stop the Democratic National Committee from formally taking a stand in favor of such benefits. Homosexual activists are also demanding that children raised by a homosexual couple be eligible for benefits when one of the partners dies—*even if the deceased partner was not the child's biological or adoptive parent.*

As another example, homosexuals who are employed by the government want to be able to name their homosexual partners as dependants in order to get the taxpayers to pay for health insurance for them. Never mind that most homosexual couples include two wage-earners, each of whom can obtain his or her own insurance. Never mind that "dependants" were, when the tax code was developed, assumed to be children and stay-at-home mothers. And never mind that homosexuals have higher rates of physical disease, mental illness, and substance abuse, leading to more medical claims and higher insurance premiums. No, all of these logical considerations must give way in the face of the demand for taxpayer subsidies of homosexual relationships.

Benefits for homosexuals are a tangle of expensive bureaucratic red tape imposed upon businesses and private organizations. Some organizations already offer "domestic partner" benefits as a matter of choice. Social conservatives have discouraged such policies, but have not attempted to forbid them by law.

Homosexual activists have not shown similar respect for freedom of choice within the marketplace. Although they proudly tout the growing numbers of corporations offering domestic partner benefits, they fail to tell the rest of the story—that a significant majority of those corporations have done so only because some government entity put a gun to their heads—not because they decided without any coercion that it would be a good business practice or the right thing to do.

The gun to the corporate head comes in the form of what is called an "equal benefits ordinance." Initiated by several cities, and eventually adopted by the entire state of California, an equal benefits ordinance says that any corporation doing business with the city (or state or other government entity) must provide benefits to its employees' homosexual partners that are fully equal to those provided to legal spouses. The price for failing to provide such "equal benefits" is simple—a complete cutoff of all government contracts. This could obviously have a huge impact on many companies, and it is this economic calculus—not the retention of good employees—that is the real reason so many companies are now toeing the homosexual line on benefits.

In fact, the coercive power of such ordinances is so great that even an evangelical Christian church organization—the Salvation Army—momentarily opened the door to providing such benefits in 2001, before an outcry from within and without caused the Salvation Army to back off and stay true to its doctrinal statements opposing homosexuality. This, however, led to the cutoff of extensive public funding for the Salvation Army's many valuable and effective social service programs— to the detriment not only of the Salvation Army, but also of the people who had benefited so greatly from those programs.

Imagine, though, what the impact on employee benefit programs would be if homosexual marriage were legalized nationwide. Right now, marriage still provides a clear, bright line, both legally and socially, to distinguish those who receive dependant benefits and those who don't. But if homosexual couples are granted the full legal status of civil marriage, then employers who do not want to grant benefits to homosexual partners—whether out of principle, like the Salvation Army, or simply out of prudent economic judgment—might be coerced by court orders to do so.

Any practice that allows more people to feed at the public trough while trampling on freedom of religion and freedom of the marketplace should be vigorously opposed by any true libertarian.

Homosexual Activists Want Judges— Not the People or Their Elected Representatives—to Make Laws

When certain "rights" need to be enshrined as part of our political system, the proper course is to amend the Constitution to make those rights explicit. The founders of our nation did that by adding the Bill of Rights to the original Constitution. The rights and freedoms of black Americans were written into the Constitution in the Thirteenth, Fourteenth, and Fifteenth

Amendments. The Nineteenth Amendment granted women the right to vote.

Therefore, if homosexual activists want to have homosexual marriage declared a fundamental right within our political system, *they* should be the ones seeking a constitutional amendment. But they are not seeking an amendment because they know it would be defeated.

Instead, the majority of the people—those who want to maintain the definition of our most fundamental social institution—have been forced to seek a constitutional amendment to protect marriage as the union of one man and one woman.

An amendment is necessary *not* because the legislatures of the respective states have begun passing laws granting same-sex civil marriages. Not a single state has passed such a law. And while a handful of states have succumbed to the pressure of the homosexual lobby and granted some of the legal rights and benefits of marriage to homosexual couples, not a single state has even done that when the decision was left to the people through a popular referendum. If there is a "groundswell" of public support for homosexual marriage, it has not yet registered on any seismometer.

No, an amendment to the Constitution to state the obvious (that marriage is between one man and one woman) is necessary because *arrogant, activist judges have taken it upon themselves to rewrite marriage law and constitutional law to fabricate a "right" to homosexual marriage*. Nothing is more anti-libertarian than judges acting as little dictators who write laws, rather than interpreting them in accordance with their obvious original intent. Such "judicial activism" is undoing the will of the people and democratic government.

In the 1990s, state supreme court justices in Alaska and Hawaii were the first to fabricate a supposed right to homosexual marriage. But the people of these states acted quickly and decisively to amend their state constitutions to prevent implementation of legal homosexual marriages. Then in Vermont, the state supreme court ruled that the state must either provide marriage licenses to homosexual couples or by some other means provide homosexual couples with the same legal rights and benefits as married couples. The Vermont legislature chose the euphemism "civil unions" to describe the homosexual-marriage-in-all-but-name it created to conform to the high court's ruling. Then on November 18, 2003, the Supreme Judicial Court of Massachusetts, by a 4–3 vote, decided that the state constitution included an unwritten and previously unnoticed right to homosexual marriage. The court ruled in February 2004 that Vermont-style civil unions were not enough.

The actions of activist judges in four states make it inevitable that homosexual marriage will lead to a federal court case, as homosexual couples married in one state will seek recognition in another. The issue will be to force all states to recognize homosexual marriages. Many observers believe that the 2003 *Lawrence v. Texas* decision could be used as precedent for a subsequent decision requiring homosexual marriage nationwide in yet another shocking example of judges rewriting democratically adopted laws to satisfy a principle that is nowhere in the text of the Constitution.

Judges have assumed the right of "judicial review," which means that they can strike down laws they believe to be in conflict with the state or federal Constitution. Even if activist state judges are reined in by amending state constitutions to define marriage as the union of one man and one woman, those provisions are vulnerable to being overturned by a decision of the U.S. Supreme Court. The only way to prevent the raw exercise of judicial power is to pass a federal constitutional amendment.

What about "States' Rights" and "Federalism?"

Homosexual activists who favor homosexual marriage often cite "states' rights" and "federalism" as arguments against a federal constitutional amendment affirming the traditional definition of marriage. Of course, the appeal to "states' rights" and "federalism" is wholly disingenuous on the part of most homosexual activists, who are not by and large conservatives in favor of limited government. Indeed, homosexual activists are fighting *against* the right of states to determine their own laws and social policies *through democratic means* when it comes to homosexual marriage. They advocate empowering liberal judicial tyranny to overturn the will of the people in the various states on this issue.

In fact, the Federal Marriage Amendment (FMA) currently before Congress not only affirms traditional marriage but respects the principle of federalism by leaving the door open for state legislatures (but not the courts) to grant some of the legal benefits of marriage to same-sex couples. In other words, the FMA is primarily a defense of democracy, not an attack upon federalism.

It is true that the FMA would define "marriage" in a way that no one state could change, even by democratic means. But here, the example of the civil rights movement works in favor of the defense of marriage, not (as is often asserted) in favor of the homosexual assault upon it. The legal problem that allowed slavery to persist until the Civil War was that we did not have a common, nationwide definition of who was a citizen or even who was a "person." That problem was rectified (in the Constitution, if not in the culture) by the Thirteenth, Fourteenth, and Fifteenth Amendments.[4] The Federal Marriage Amendment would serve a similar purpose, because "marriage," like "personhood" and "citizenship," is a concept so fundamental to our society that we cannot succeed as a nation with multiple definitions of its meaning.

While it is true that the federal government has generally deferred to the states on marriage law, the one significant exception was over the definition of marriage. When Utah sought admission to the union as a state, Congress declared that the territory would first have to legally renounce the practice of polygamy—indeed, the Utah territory would have to expressly forbid it. Utah eventually agreed to these terms (which were also upheld by the U.S. Supreme Court).

Other People Who Should Support the Federal Marriage Amendment

Democrats

Democratic politicians have one very good reason for supporting a clear definition of marriage as the union of one man and one woman—it is supported by a majority, not just of all voters, but by *a majority of Democratic voters as well*. As reported by columnist Maggie Gallagher, "55 percent of *Democrats* support a constitutional amendment defining marriage."[5]

Apart from the poll numbers, there is good reason in principle why Democrats should oppose same-sex marriage. Democrats have always prided themselves on being champions of the "little guy." Of course, homosexual activists are diligent about presenting themselves as an oppressed minority group worthy of Democratic sympathy. But the real "little guys" liberals should be worried about are not well-heeled homosexual activists but America's children. Homosexual marriage would further separate marriage from its natural role in producing and nurturing children. That separation would mean more children growing up in motherless or fatherless homes and suffering higher rates of poverty, criminality, and various social pathologies.

Many Democrats understand this. Even in liberal Massachusetts—and I speak as a former liberal Democratic activist in Massachusetts—the overwhelming majority of Democrats in the legislature support an amendment to the state constitution to define marriage as the union of one man and one woman.[6]

Women

Polls show that among women, as among Democrats, a majority favors the historic definition of marriage, but by a smaller percentage than in the population as a whole. It can well be argued, however, that women have more to lose from homosexual marriage than do men.

Many anthropologists believe that marriage developed in primitive societies as a way of "taming" men. Marriage continues to be an effective institution to protect women, both by tying men to a monogamous relationship that protects children and gives them a stable family and by putting men to work on behalf of the children and their mother.

"If America normalizes male homosexuality through gay marriage," writes anthropology professor Peter Wood of Boston University, the general results are predictable: "the status of women as mothers will further erode,"[7] because children and motherhood will no longer be the centerpiece of marriage.

Another problem for women is that as the ultimate legal and social affirmation of homosexuality, homosexual civil marriage might encourage more men to adopt a homosexual lifestyle,[8] as it offers sex without responsibility. Given that surveys show that twice as many men are homosexual as are women,[9] such a development is only going to make the problem of "too few men to go around" even worse.

Men

While it may seem incongruous that I would argue that men are hurt by homosexual marriage immediately after arguing that women are hurt by it, it is really quite logical. The fundamental logic of natural marriage is that men and women need each other. The fundamental logic of homosexual marriage denies that and by implication denies the role of fatherhood. America already has a crisis of broken families with men refusing to be responsible fathers. Homosexual marriage will make the problem worse.

Columnist Maggie Gallagher has recounted sitting on an airplane next to a young man with whom she began talking about her work in defense of marriage (and against homosexual marriage). To make her point, she asked if he didn't think children need both mothers and fathers. "Not really," he replied. "I don't think so." Gallagher then tried to make the issue more personal. "What about you?" she asked. "Do you think you'll matter to your kids?" He thought a moment, then replied, "No. Not really." It was an answer that was honest and consistent—but also fatalistic and telling.[10]

Children suffer without fathers. Boys lose a vital male role model. And adult men themselves lose the maturity that comes with accepting the responsibilities of fatherhood.[11]

Homosexuals

This might seem the most counterintuitive argument of all. Yet the fact is that many homosexuals in the past have not supported the notion of homosexual marriage, and many still do not today.

Homosexuals opposed to homosexual marriage fall largely into two camps. One consists of those who see homosexuality as countercultural and rebellious by its very nature, and want no part of an institution they see as archaic, patriarchal, and clearly designed to meet the needs of heterosexuals, not gay people.[12]

Other homosexuals oppose homosexual marriage not because it poses a threat to the libertine homosexual lifestyle, but because they are intellectually honest enough to recognize the unique contribution to human society that is made by marriage between a man and a woman. Canadian scholar Paul Nathanson of McGill University is perhaps the most articulate of these. I heard him speak at an academic conference in Atlanta in March 2003. The gist of his remarks is worth quoting at length.

Nathanson and his colleague Katherine Young begin by not-ing that "the *burden of proof* is always on those who want *change*," (in this case, the advocates of homosexual marriage) and they ask, "Why take the risk of a massive experiment?" They then come to the heart of their argument:

Because heterosexuality is directly related to both reproduction and survival, ... *every* human societ[y] has had to *promote* it actively.... This has always required a massive cultural effort involving theology or myths, rituals, rewards, privileges, and so on. Heterosexuality is always *fostered* by a cultural norm, in other words, not merely allowed as one "lifestyle choice" among many. The result ... is a "privileged" status for heterosexuality. Postmodernists are not wrong in identifying it as such, but they *are* wrong in assuming that any society can do without it.

To be more specific, culture must do at least five things: (a) foster the bonding between men and women in order to pro-vide an appropriate setting for maturing children and to ensure the cooperation of men and women for the common good; (b) foster the bonding between men and children so that men are likely to become active participants in family life; (c) foster the birth and rearing of children, at least to the extent necessary for preserving and fostering society, in culturally approved ways (an obvious example being the prohibition of incest); (d) fos-ter some healthy form of masculine identity—that is, an iden-tity based on at least one distinctive, necessary, and publicly valued contribution to society (responsible fatherhood being one obvious example); and (e) foster the transformation of ado-lescents into sexually responsible adults.

Nathanson and Young also note an important pattern: "Marriage has universal, nearly universal, and variable features." The failure to understand this accounts for the illogic of some advocates of homosexual marriage, who take changes in some of the *variable* features of marriage (such as the payment of a dowry) as precedent for destroying one of its *universal* features—the male-female union. Nathanson and Young say:

> Its *universal* features include the fact that marriage is (a) supported by authority and incentives; (b) recognizes the interdependence of men and women; (c) has a public dimension; (d) defines eligible partners; (e) encourages procreation under specific conditions; and (f) provides mutual support not only between men and women but also between them and their children.[13]

If all homosexuals were as reasonable and rational as Paul Nathanson, there would be no "culture war" over gay marriage.

3

Is Rosie O'Donnell the New Rosa Parks?

THE CIVIL RIGHTS ARGUMENTS

One of the homosexuals who traveled to San Francisco to receive an illegal marriage license from Mayor Gavin Newsom put it succinctly: "I am tired of sitting at the back of the bus."[1]

The allusion, of course, was to the famous story of Rosa Parks. Parks is the African American woman who in 1955 boarded a bus in Montgomery, Alabama, sat down near the front, and refused the driver's order to move to the back of the bus, as African Americans were required to do under "Jim Crow" racial segregation laws.

Parks's arrest sparked the Montgomery bus boycott, in which Montgomery's African American population, led by a young minister named Martin Luther King Jr., stopped riding the city's buses (thus crippling the bus system financially) until the city agreed to fully integrate the buses. The Montgomery bus boycott is generally viewed as the beginning of the great civil rights movement of the 1950s and 1960s, which culminated legislatively in the passage of the Civil Rights Act of 1964, banning racial discrimination in employment, housing, and public accommodations.

The stories of Rosa Parks and Martin Luther King Jr. have become an inspiring part of American history. So it's not surprising that homosexual activists have tried to hitch their caboose to the civil rights train. Sexual orientation is a very different category than race, and African Americans themselves reject the comparison.

Defining Terms:
What Are "Civil Rights," Anyway?

If you ask an average person what the term "civil rights" means, you're likely to get an answer like this: "It means everyone is treated equally," or "It means getting rid of discrimination."

The dictionary defines civil rights as "rights belonging to a person by virtue of his status as a citizen or as a member of civil society."[2] The Bill of Rights in the United States Constitution guarantees that every American has the right to freedom of religion, speech, and the press; as well as "due process of law;" protections against unreasonable search and seizure; "double jeopardy" (being tried twice for the same crime); and self-incrimination.

These are true "civil" rights in that they belong to every person "as a citizen or as a member of civil society." But please note well—*homosexuals have never been denied any of these rights, nor is anyone proposing to deny such rights to homosexuals in the future.*

When homosexual activists talk about their "civil rights," they are not talking about their constitutional rights, which have never been denied to them (unlike the historical experience of black Americans). Instead, they are talking about "civil rights" in the sense that the term was used in the Civil Rights Act of 1964, which laid down that it was illegal to practice discrimination on the basis of race, color, national origin, or religion.[3] What do these protected categories have in common?

The answer is that the law grants protection against "discrimination" on the basis of personal characteristics that are:

- Inborn, involuntary, and immutable (like race and color)
- Innocuous (because they do no harm to the person's ability to do the job, pay the rent, and so on, and do no harm to society as a whole)
- In the Constitution

Now we come to the key question. Is "sexual orientation," like race and sex, a characteristic that is inborn, involuntary, immutable, innocuous, and in the Constitution? Is it, like religion (which is not inborn, involuntary, immutable, or innocuous, but is in the Constitution), a characteristic that meets even *one* of these criteria?

The only truthful answer is no.

Is homosexuality inborn?

I must be quite blunt here. The notion that people are "born gay" is nothing less than The Big Lie of the entire homosexual movement. Science has not proven that there is a "gay gene" or that people are "born gay." The widespread belief that there is a "gay gene" can largely be traced to the publicity surrounding three scientific studies in the early 1990s: one studying brains, one studying twins, and one studying genes.

THE BRAIN STUDY

In 1991, following the death of his homosexual lover from AIDS, researcher Simon LeVay decided to search the brains of cadavers to find a physical determinant for homosexuality.[4] He examined the size of a brain structure known as INAH3, which has been linked to sexual behavior in animals, in the cadavers of six women (who were presumed to be heterosexual) and thirty-five men—eighteen known to have been homosexual, one known to have been bisexual, and sixteen presumed to have been heterosexual. LeVay reported that INAH3 was larger in heterosexual men than in heterosexual women, but also larger in heterosexual men than in homosexual men. This result, LeVay concluded, "suggests that sexual orientation has a biological substrate."[5]

Other researchers, however, had numerous problems with this interpretation. For example, six of the sixteen supposedly "heterosexual" male subjects had died of AIDS—an extraordinarily large percentage. As one analyst put it, "[I]t seems quite possible that LeVay... classified some homosexuals as heterosexuals."[6]

Other problems included the significant overlap in the overall range of INAH3 sizes between the "homosexual" and "heterosexual" groups, the possibility that sexual behavior could influence brain structure (rather than vice versa), and the possibility that the observed effect was a result of AIDS (which caused the death of all of LeVay's "homosexual" subjects), rather than a determinant of sexual orientation as such.[7]

A critique in the *Archives of General Psychiatry* concluded that this and two other studies of brain structures remain "as yet uncorroborated" and "must be viewed cautiously while replication studies are pending." It further noted that even if such studies are replicated, "we will not know whether the anatomic correlates are a cause or a consequence of sexual orientation."[8]

THE TWINS STUDY

The twins study was conducted by J. Michael Bailey and Richard C. Pillard. Bailey and Pillard sought to identify homosexuals who had an identical twin. They then surveyed the sexual orientation of these twins. They theorized that if identical twins share the trait of homosexuality at a rate higher than, say, fraternal twins, non-twin siblings, or adoptive siblings, then that could be taken as evidence of a genetic component in homosexuality. In their study, they found that when one identical twin was homosexual, 52 percent of the time his identical twin was homosexual as well. Since this was a "concordance" rate much higher than among other siblings, they took this as confirmation of the theory of a genetic component in homosexuality.[9]

This study had problems too, is contradicted by other studies, and falls down on its own evidence. On this last point, if you did a study of identical twins, you would find that one hundred percent of black identical twins would be black, one hundred percent of male identical twins would be male, one hundred percent of redheaded identical twins would be redheads, and one hundred percent of blue-eyed identical twins would have blue eyes. Remember, identical twins (known to scientists as "dizygotic," meaning that they come from the same fertilized egg) have a completely, one hundred percent identical genetic makeup. Therefore, a study showing that 52 percent of the identical twins of homosexuals are also homosexual proves only one thing—that homosexuality is not genetic.

Similar twin studies have not found a concordance rate for homosexuality that is anywhere near as high as 50 percent. For example, a more recent study of twins in Minnesota found "no significant genetic effects" on sexual orientation among males, some effect among females, but with an overall conclusion that "environmental effects were . . . more important in the aggregate than genetic effects."[10]

Bailey and Pillard made no effort to control for environment in the development of their twin subjects. In other words, this was not a classic study of twins separated at birth. The twins studied were raised in the same home, and given that they were identical in age, appearance, natural talents and dispositions, and so on, it is not surprising that their environment and experiences (including ones that might influence the development of homosexuality) would be more similar than non-identical or non-twin siblings. The analysis by William Byne and Bruce Parsons in the *Archives of General Psychiatry* noted that this factor—the "increased similarity of the trait-relevant environment" for the identical twins—could mean that "any difference in the true concordance rates would be attributable to environmental rather than genetic factors."[11]

THE GENE STUDY

Only one of the three most famous "gay gene" studies actually looked directly at genes. This was the 1993 study by Dean

Hamer, a geneticist with the National Cancer Institute. Studying patterns of male homosexuality in extended families, he found a correlation between the existence of homosexual brothers and homosexuality among maternal uncles and other male relatives on the maternal side. From this, he theorized the existence of a gene influencing the development of homosexuality that is transmitted through the maternal line (that is, on the X chromosome, which men inherit from their mothers). Hamer then examined DNA from these related men, and claimed to have found "a gene that contributes to homosexual orientation in males" at a location called Xq28.[12]

This supposed discovery of a "gay gene" made headlines. Hamer's numerous caveats were less widely reported. For instance, Hamer noted that "the observed rates of homosexual orientation . . . were lower than would be expected for a simple Mendelian [i.e., directly inherited] trait."[13] He also admitted that not all cases of homosexuality could be explained by this gene marker,[14] and that no conclusion could be drawn as to what percentage of homosexuality might have a genetic link.[15] Finally, Hamer said there was a need to identify "environmental, experiential, or cultural factors . . . that influence the development of male sexual orientation."[16]

Even with those qualifying remarks, however, Hamer's finding remains suspect for one key reason—other scientists have been unable to replicate it, a key step in declaring any scientific finding to be "proven." A team of researchers led by George Rice, writing in the journal *Science* in 1999, reported on an attempt to confirm Hamer's findings. "Because our study was larger than that of Hamer et al.," they reported, "we certainly had adequate power to detect a genetic effect as large as was reported in that study."[17] Nevertheless, the Rice study's "results do not support an X-linked gene underlying male homosexuality."[18]

Scientists who have reviewed the data regarding biological or genetic theories on the origin of homosexuality have concluded that "the appeal of current biologic explanations for sexual orientation may derive more from dissatisfaction with the present status of psychosocial explanations than from a substantiating body of experimental data. Critical review shows the evidence favoring a biologic theory to be lacking."[19]

Conclusion: The scientific evidence shows that homosexuality is *not* inborn.

Is homosexuality involuntary?

There are three aspects to "sexual orientation": attraction, behavior, and self-identification.

Attractions are indeed "involuntary." But people choose, and can be held responsible for, what overt sexual behaviors they actually engage in. A heterosexual married man might feel sexually attracted to a woman who is not his wife, but if he acts on that attraction, he is rightly condemned for an act of adultery. The fact that his sexual attraction was "involuntary" is no excuse for failing to control his actual behavior.

Homosexuals complain, however, that in effect they are being asked to refrain from sex altogether. But this argument only makes sense if homosexuals are utterly incapable of engaging in heterosexual relationships—a contention not borne out by the research.

According to the 1994 National Health and Social Life Survey, the most comprehensive national survey of sexuality ever conducted, 2.8 percent of American adult men and 1.4 percent of American adult women identify themselves as homosexuals.[20] But the same survey showed that only 0.6 percent of men and 0.2 percent of women report having had only same-sex sexual experiences since puberty.[21] In other words, about 80 percent of self-identified "homosexuals" have engaged in heterosexual relationships.

So homosexual attractions might indeed be involuntary, but such attractions are psychological, invisible, and secret, and therefore essentially irrelevant to public policy. Homosexual behavior (and the desire of homosexual activists to have official government affirmation of such behavior) is what is really relevant to the debate over the definition of marriage. And since such behavior is clearly voluntary, the criterion for civil rights protection of homosexuality as an "involuntary" characteristic thus does not apply.

Is homosexuality immutable?

There is no such thing as a former black person, nor, despite sex-change surgery, is there such a thing as a former woman or a former man, if chromosomes are the measure of one's gender identity. There are, however, thousands of former homosexuals.

The strongest scientific evidence of this was provided by one of the most unlikely sources. Robert L. Spitzer is a psychiatrist who was instrumental in pushing for the American Psychiatric Association's controversial 1973 decision to remove homosexuality from its list of mental disorders. That event was a crucial early victory for homosexual activists, on which much of the subsequent success of their agenda has rested.

Nevertheless, Dr. Spitzer had the intellectual honesty to accept a challenge to study the results of what is called "reparative therapy" for homosexuality. Reparative therapy is a mental health treatment designed to reduce unwanted urges and behavior.

Dr. Spitzer studied two hundred people who had reported some measure of change from a homosexual to a heterosexual orientation. Each of his subjects participated in a structured interview consisting of 114 questions. The study identified ten different measures of "sexual orientation," ranging from sexual attractions to self-identification to sexual fantasies to actual sexual behavior, as well as three separate measures of purported heterosexual functioning.[22]

Spitzer published his conclusions in 2003:

This study indicates that some gay men and lesbians, following reparative therapy, report that they have made major changes from a predominantly homosexual orientation to a predominantly heterosexual orientation. The changes following reparative therapy were not limited to sexual behavior and sexual orientation self-identity. The changes encompassed sexual attraction, arousal, fantasy, yearning, and being bothered by homosexual feelings. The changes encompassed the core aspects of sexual orientation.[23]

So much for homosexuality being immutable.

That is not to say that changing from a homosexual to a heterosexual orientation is easy. The Spitzer study tells us nothing about the percentage of people who begin such therapy who arrive at a successful outcome. Just like any other therapy designed to change deeply rooted attitudes and behavior patterns, reparative therapy for homosexuality is undoubtedly difficult. But the argument of homosexual activists is not that such change is difficult; they insist that it is impossible. A survey of the literature in 2001, however, found at least nineteen studies with tangible data suggesting that a homosexual orientation can be changed.[24]

Is homosexuality innocuous?

With respect to race, virtually everyone would agree that the mere color of a person's skin, in and of itself, cannot rationally be viewed as posing a threat to society. With respect to sex, not only are males and females equal in essential value, but the existence of both is necessary for the survival of society. But can one say the same about homosexuality?

Arguing that homosexual relationships enrich people's personal lives in the same way that heterosexual ones do, some advocates of homosexual marriage openly claim, as writer Andrew Sullivan did in a recent public forum, that "homosexuality... is a moral good."[25] But there is considerable evidence that homosexuality causes tangible harms and imposes significant costs on society. I am defining "homosexuality" here as "overt sexual acts committed between persons of the same sex." I believe this is the definition most relevant to the homosexual marriage debate, since this is what society is being asked expressly to affirm.

In fact, there is considerable evidence that homosexual behavior is associated with higher rates of:

- Promiscuity
- Sexually transmitted diseases
- Mental illness
- Substance abuse
- Domestic violence
- Child sexual abuse

Let's look at each of these in turn.

HOMOSEXUAL PROMISCUITY

Studies indicate that the average homosexual male has hundreds of sex partners in his lifetime.

- A. P. Bell and M. S. Weinberg, in their classic 1978 study of male and female homosexuality, found that 43 percent of white homosexual males had sex with five hundred or more partners, with 28 percent having one thousand or more sex partners.[26]
- In a study of the sexual profiles of 2,583 older homosexual men published in the *Journal of Sex Research*, Paul Van de Ven and others found that "the modal range for number of sexual partners ever [of homosexual men] was 101–500." In addition, 10.2 percent to 15.7 percent had between 501 and one thousand partners. A smaller percentage reported having had more than one thousand lifetime sexual partners.[27]

Startlingly, lesbians have higher rates of promiscuity as well—with men.

- The journal *Sexually Transmitted Infections* found that "the median number of lifetime male sexual partners was significantly greater for WSW (women who have sex with women) than controls (twelve partners versus six). WSW were significantly more likely to report more than fifty lifetime male sexual partners."[28]

SEXUALLY TRANSMITTED DISEASES

- Fifty-two percent of the cumulative total of AIDS cases in the United States are known to have been in men who have sex with men,[29] even though only 5.3 percent of American men have had sex with another man even once since age eighteen.[30]

- Even the Gay and Lesbian Medical Association acknowledges, "Sexually transmitted diseases (STDs) occur in sexually active gay men at a high rate." The association's website notes that these include STD infections "for which no cure is available (HIV, Hepatitis A, B, or C virus, Human Papillomavirus, etc.)."[31]

- The journal *Sexually Transmitted Infections* also reported "a higher prevalence of BV (bacterial vaginosis), hepatitis C, and HIV risk behaviors in WSW [women who have sex with women] as compared with controls."[32]

MENTAL ILLNESS

- A study in the *Archives of General Psychiatry* found that gay, lesbian, and bisexual young people were at increased risk for major depression, generalized anxiety disorder, conduct disorder, multiple disorders, suicidal ideation, and suicide attempts.[33]

SUBSTANCE ABUSE

- The Gay and Lesbian Medical Association (GLMA) says, "Gay men use substances at a higher rate than the general population, and not just in larger communities such as New York, San Francisco, and Los Angeles." They add that evidence suggests that "gay men have higher rates of alcohol dependence and abuse than straight men," and "gay men use tobacco at much higher rates than straight men."[34]

- The GLMA also reports that "illicit drugs may be used more often among lesbians than heterosexual women;" that "tobacco and smoking products may be used more often by lesbians than by heterosexual women;" and that alcohol "use and abuse may be higher among lesbians."[35]

DOMESTIC VIOLENCE

- A study in the *Journal of Interpersonal Violence* examined conflict and violence in lesbian relationships. The researchers found that 90 percent of the lesbians surveyed had been recipients of one or more acts of verbal aggression from their intimate partners during the year prior to this study, with 31 percent reporting one or more incidents of physical abuse.[36]

- In their book *Men Who Beat the Men Who Love Them: Battered Gay Men and Domestic Violence*, authors Island and Letellier estimate that "the incidence of domestic violence among gay men is nearly double that in the heterosexual population."[37]

CHILD SEXUAL ABUSE

No one would make the case that all or even most homosexuals are pedophiles or even potential pedophiles, but it is unfortunately true that existing evidence suggests that male pedophilia is disproportionately homosexual.

- Significant numbers of victims are males: A study of 457 male sex offenders against children in *Journal of Sex & Marital Therapy* found that "approximately one-third of these sexual offenders directed their sexual activity against males."[38] A study in the *Journal of Sex Research* found that although heterosexuals outnumber homosexuals by a ratio of at least 20 to 1, homosexual pedophiles commit about one-third of the total number of child sex offenses.[39]
- Many pedophiles consider themselves to be homosexual: A study of 229 convicted child molesters in *Archives of Sexual Behavior* found that "86 percent of offenders against males described themselves as homosexual or bisexual."[40]

There is nothing innocuous about these noxious pathologies.

Is homosexuality in the Constitution?

It almost goes without saying that there is no reference to homosexuality or to "sexual orientation" (or, for that matter, to sex or marriage at all) in the U.S. Constitution. *Lawrence v. Texas* notwithstanding, there is not the tiniest shred of evidence that the founding fathers ever intended their work to protect homosexual acts of any kind, let alone create a right to homosexual "marriage."

In fact, the historical record shows the founding fathers considered homosexual acts an abominable crime. Just weeks after the Declaration of Independence, Thomas Jefferson wrote in a letter that "buggery" (homosexual sodomy) should be punished "by castration." While at Valley Forge in 1778, General George Washington drummed out of his army a soldier who had attempted to commit sodomy with another, declaring his "abhorrence and detestation of such infamous crimes."[41]

In summary, homosexual behavior is not inborn, involuntary, immutable, or innocuous, nor is it found in the Constitution. There is no basis for treating it as a protected category under civil rights laws, or for granting special protection against "discrimination" based on sexual orientation.

What Do African Americans Say about the "Civil Rights" Argument for Homosexual "Marriage?"

There are certainly some prominent African Americans who fully endorse the analogy that homosexual activists make between the black civil rights movement of the 1950s and 1960s and the current push for homosexual marriage. Most significant, perhaps, is Coretta Scott King, the widow of the late Rev. Dr. Martin Luther King Jr., who reportedly declared in a March 2004 speech that "gay and lesbian . . . families should have legal protection, whether by marriage or civil union."[42]

Also supporting the homosexual marriage/civil rights analogy is Democratic congressman John Lewis of Georgia, who spoke as a young man at the famous 1963 March on Washington for civil rights. He has written, "I have fought too hard and too long against discrimination based on race and color not to stand up against discrimination based on sexual orientation."[43] Both black candidates for president in 2004, Carol Moseley Braun and Al Sharpton, endorsed homosexual marriage, positioning themselves to the left of their white counterparts in the Democratic field, most of whom (apart from Dennis Kucinich) endorse civil unions but not civil marriage for homosexuals.[44] And one black Democratic state senator, Dianne Wilkerson, endorsed the civil rights analogy in an emotional speech during the debate over a constitutional amendment on marriage in Massachusetts. Wilkerson declared, "I know the pain of being less than equal, and I cannot and will not impose that status on anyone else."[45]

Polling data clearly indicates, however, that these black spokesmen do not represent the dominant viewpoint among African Americans. On the contrary, it is clear that blacks not only oppose homosexual marriage, but do so by a larger margin than whites. For example, a poll released by the Pew Research Center for the People and the Press on November 18, 2003, (the same day as the *Goodridge* decision legalizing homosexual marriage in Massachusetts) found that 60 percent of African Americans oppose homosexual marriage.[46] A Gallup poll taken in February 2004 found that a majority of African Americans support a federal marriage amendment. The findings are the same at the statewide level. For example, in California, our largest state, the *Los Angeles Times* exit poll after Election Day 2000 found that African Americans supported Proposition 22, which limits marriage in California to unions of one man and one woman, by a larger margin than did whites or Asian Americans.

A Field poll in California in February 2004 found the same—that African Americans oppose homosexual marriage and support a constitutional amendment to ban it by wider margins than do other ethnic groups.[47]

The liberal magazine *The Nation* reported on another poll in October 2003 this way:

> All the national polls show that the lower down voters are on the education and income scales, the more antigay they are; thus, blacks oppose gay marriage by a whopping 65 to 28 percent, while among Hispanics it's 54 to 40 percent, according to an August *New York Times* poll.[48]

This comment drew an angry response from Tracey Lee, an African American attorney in Michigan:

> What this man is clearly saying is that African-Americans and Hispanics oppose homosexual marriage because, according to him, we're too dumb and too poor to know any better.... The blatant racism of such a patronizing slander is matched only by its arrogance.... [I am]surprised that a respected magazine with a liberal viewpoint would publish such a racially insensitive and obviously bigoted characterization.[49]

One reason blacks are angry at homosexuals' usurpation of the "civil rights" label is that they see no comparison between the historical experience of African Americans and the current situation of homosexuals. "When the homosexual compares himself to the black community, he doesn't know what suffering is," said Clarence James, an African American studies professor at Temple University.[50] The Reverend Talbert Swan II said, "For me to walk down the street and get profiled just because of my skin color is something a homosexual will never go through."[51] An article in the *Sacramento Bee* noted that other blacks "look at the weak economic state of their communities and bridle at the push for civil rights by a segment of the population whose neighborhoods often are in much better shape."[52]

George E. Curry, editor in chief of BlackPressUSA.com, summarizes this point at greater length:

> Gays and lesbians have never suffered anything approaching the oppression of African Americans. They were not lynched because they were gay, they were not brought here in chains because of their sexual orientation, they were not deprived of the right to vote because they like people of the same gender, and no White girl in the United States has ever been killed for whistling at a White woman.[53]

One of the most prominent black advocates for traditional, or natural, marriage has been Walter E. Fauntroy, one of the organizers of the 1963 March on Washington, who later served as the District of Columbia's delegate in the U.S. House of Representatives. "For most black Americans who know our history, we do not want any further confusion about what a marriage and family happens to be," says Fauntroy. "We have not yet recovered from the cruelties of slavery, which were based on the destruction of the family."[54]

Star Parker, president of the Coalition on Urban Renewal and Education, expanded upon this theme. "Forty years ago, 70 percent of black families were intact, with husband and wife together. Out of wedlock births were a third of what they are today," she noted. Today, the picture is far different:

- 60 percent of black children grow up in fatherless homes
- 70 percent of black babies are born to unwed mothers
- More than 300,000 black babies are aborted annually
- 50 percent of new AIDS cases are in the black community

In Parker's view:

> The prodigious challenge that the black community faces today is to restore the black family and to revitalize the values and traditions that will keep those families together and enable them to raise emotionally and spiritually healthy productive children.... The last thing we need at this point is the legal marginalization of our traditional values, which is what the gay community wants.[55]

Not *Loving* It

One "civil rights" argument that has gained considerable traction in the debate over homosexual marriage is the comparison to states banning interracial marriage.

Such laws were finally overturned by the U.S. Supreme Court in 1967, in a case called (rather poetically) *Loving v. Virginia*. Richard Loving, a white man, had married Mildred Jeter Loving, a black woman, in the District of Columbia. They later moved to Virginia. In 1958, police officers entered their house in the middle of the night and demanded to know, "What are you doing in bed with this lady?" Although the Lovings had their marriage certificate hanging on the wall, the sheriff was unimpressed, declaring, "That's no good here." The couple was jailed for five days, after which a judge accepted their guilty plea to a charge of violating the state's anti-miscegenation statute. They were given the choice of spending a year in jail or leaving the state. They chose to return to D.C. and then filed suit to overturn their conviction. The Lovings were vindicated by a unanimous Supreme Court nine years later.[56] The Court ruled that "the freedom of choice to marry [cannot] be restricted by invidious racial discrimination."[57]

California's supreme court had already struck down a similar statute nineteen years earlier. That court had declared that "the essence of the right to marry is freedom to join in marriage with the person of one's choice."[58] Homosexual activists claim that this is precisely the principle that should apply to their efforts to marry a chosen person of the same sex. There is a certain logic to this argument. Laws against same-sex marriage do restrict a person's choice of marriage partner, as did laws against interracial marriage. But the flaw in the argument is that no one—not even the most radical advocate of homosexual marriage—is proposing to eliminate all restrictions on one's choice of marriage partner. Every state forbids marriage to specific classes of people—namely, those who are already married, children, or certain close blood relatives.

The point, then, of the cases on interracial marriage cannot have been that restrictions on marital choice are unacceptable across the board. It was, rather, more specifically that *race* was not a legitimate basis for imposing such a restriction. Indeed, the U.S. Supreme Court in *Loving* did not make quite as sweeping a statement about marital choice as the California court. Instead, it said that "the freedom of choice to marry [cannot] be restricted by invidious racial discrimination."[59]

The reason for this was described in a 2003 Indiana court decision rejecting the claim of a right to homosexual marriage. As the judge noted, "Anti-miscegenation laws, because they interfered with the traditional marriage relationships in pursuit of opprobrious racial segregation policies, had no legitimate connection to the institution of marriage itself.... whatever else marriage is about, it is not about racial segregation." In contrast, however, "restrictions against same-sex marriage reinforces, rather than disrupts, the traditional understanding of marriage as a unique relationship between a woman and a man. Marriage traditionally and definitionally has had to do with the sex of each participant."[60]

A superior court in New Jersey came to a similar conclusion in a 2003 case:

Plaintiffs' reliance on decisions striking down statutes that prohibit interracial marriage is misplaced. These decisions derive from Constitutional amendments prohibiting racial discrimination and subjecting laws that classify individuals based on race to the highest level of scrutiny. No similar Constitutional provisions outlaw statutory classifications based on sexual orientation.... Comparing the State's marriage statutes to laws perpetuating racial prejudice, therefore, is inapposite.

Individuals challenging bans on interracial marriage had a powerful weapon: Federal Constitutional provisions, passed by

Congress and adopted by State Legislatures, that expressly prohibited States from denying recognized rights based on race. It was entirely appropriate for the courts to enforce those duly enacted Constitutional provisions by striking down statutes that made race a qualifying condition for access to a recognized right to marry. Plaintiffs, on the other hand, assert their claims in the absence of express Constitutional provisions supporting their position, and ask the court to circumvent the Legislative process by creating a right that has never before been recognized in this country.

The mandate for racial equality is firmly enshrined in both the Federal and State Constitutions. Importantly, two amendments [the Thirteenth and Fourteenth] to the United States Constitution expressly address racial equality. . . .

The Supreme Court's decision in *Loving v. Virginia* is predicated entirely on the Fourteenth Amendment's prohibition of racial classifications. . . .

No similar Constitutional provision accords heightened protection to individuals who claim that statutes discriminate on the basis of sexual orientation. . . .

[P]laintiffs . . . lack the significant legal foundation that was available to the plaintiffs in *Loving* to demand judicial recognition of the rights they seek.[61]

Natural Marriage Builds Bridges, Not Walls

The clear purpose of the bans on interracial marriage was to build walls between two groups of people in society: blacks and whites. Such laws were designed to reinforce a system of racial segregation, keeping the races apart.

In contrast, defining marriage as the union of male and female has exactly the opposite intent and effect. Rather than building walls between two classes of people, it creates a bridge across the most fundamental gap in humanity—the gap between male and female. Bridging the divide of the sexes by uniting men and women in marriage is common to all human civilizations, and serves the good of society.

Interracial marriage does not change the definition of marriage, and laws against interracial marriage had as their only purpose preserving a social system of racial segregation.

Homosexual "marriage," on the other hand, changes the fundamental definition of the institution, and would form at least three segregated forms of marriage: male-only unions, female-only unions, and opposite-sex unions.

Banning the "marriage" of same-sex couples does not burden the institution of marriage. Instead, it preserves marriage's nature and purpose. Homosexual marriage is not a "civil right." It is a political demand that should be denied.

4

"The Laws of Nature" and the Public Purpose of Marriage

When the United States of America first saw fit to declare its independence from Great Britain, the decision was not rooted merely in personal whim or desire. Nor was it a mere exercise of raw political power. Thomas Jefferson's Declaration of Independence appealed, instead, to "the Laws of Nature and of Nature's God." This "natural law" tradition lies at the heart of what America is. It also lies at the heart of the central issue in the gay marriage debate—the question of *what marriage is*.

Homosexual activists insist that the debate is only about "civil marriage" (not religious ceremonies) so marriage can be defined in any way the public—or a court—chooses to define it. The fact is, though, that civil marriage exists merely to recognize a pre-existing social institution. The state does not create marriage—it merely recognizes it. Marriage, in its truest sense, is neither a civil institution nor a religious one, but a natural institution. The complementarity of male and female is an essential part of its nature. One can no more redefine natural marriage to exclude either male or female than one can redefine "grape juice" to exclude grapes.

For the most part, though, homosexual activists prefer to frame the debate in terms of "rights," "equality," "discrimination," or "equal access," terms that automatically predispose the listener to sympathize with advocates of homosexual marriage on grounds of "fairness" and "justice." In other words, they frame the debate as a question of access to marriage. Marriage, in this view, is a public institution to which an entire class of citizens—gay and lesbian Americans—are being denied access.

But strictly speaking, Americans who choose to self-identify as gay or lesbian already have precisely the same rights (as individuals) of access to marriage as anyone else—but subject to exactly the same terms, which include compliance with the fundamental definition of marriage as the union of male and female. Therefore, what homosexual activists are really seeking is not to expand "access" to marriage, but to change its fundamental definition.

On occasion, though, the advocates of homosexual marriage do take on the issue of the "definition" of marriage. When they do, the essence of their appeal is this: "Gay and lesbian Americans want to get married for the same reasons that anyone else does. They fall in love, and want to share their lives together, supporting one another emotionally and economically, and in some cases raise children together."

When framed in this way, it appears (as it is calculated to appear) as though these are the same reasons why opposite-sex couples get married—for love, to share life, for mutual support and maybe (but not necessarily) for children.

But this reasoning is wrong, because the private purposes for which people make the choice to enter long-term partnered relationships are essentially irrelevant to the definition of the public institution of marriage. The key question is not, "What are the reasons private individuals choose to marry?" but rather, "Why is marriage a public institution at all?"[1]

Love and companionship are not the business of government. Would we even tolerate the government issuing licenses and regulating entry and exit into relationships the only or even principal purpose of which is emotional attachment? No. Marriage is a public institution because it facilitates the union of men and women in reproducing the human race and the cooperation of mothers and fathers in raising and nurturing the children produced by their union.

Homosexual activists, of course, have a simple answer to this. They argue that because elderly, infertile, or heterosexual couples who don't want children are permitted to marry, so should homosexual couples.

True, the public interest in childless marriages is not as great as the public interest in marriages that produce children, but limiting marriage to fertile heterosexual couples who intend to have children would require an oppressive government bureaucracy. Do we want the government to ask every young couple applying for a marriage license about their intention to have children? Not only would this be a significant invasion of the couple's privacy, it is a question that many couples couldn't answer. Apart from the question of the couple's intent, do we want the state evaluating a couple's fertility? Do we want to deny marriage to post-menopausal women? Do we want to deny older men—still capable of conceiving children—wives their own age? Even couples who discover that they are infertile are capable of adopting children and providing them with the love of both a mother and a father.

Rather than determine eligibility for marriage in terms of the actual procreative intent or capacity of any one couple, we simply define the structure of marriage as being open to the entire class of couples that are even theoretically capable of natural reproduction—namely, opposite-sex ones—and we exclude an entire class of couples that are intrinsically infertile—namely, same-sex ones. Drawing the line in this way is not at all arbitrary—it is simple logic.

Now, some homosexual couples do raise children who have been conceived through artificial reproductive technologies, and some homosexual couples have adopted children. But any child brought up in the home of a homosexual couple is deliberately denied what he or she needs most—the love of both a father and a mother who are committed to one another in marriage.

The truth is that many children of homosexuals are not the product of artificial reproductive technologies, nor are they adopted. Instead, they are the biological children of one of the homosexual partners who was previously in a heterosexual relationship or marriage. Not only do these children suffer the trauma of divorce, they suffer the trauma of living in a household headed by two mothers or two fathers.

The argument in favor of same-sex marriage can only be logically sustained if one argues that there is no difference between men and women—that is, if one argues not merely that men and women are equal in value and dignity, a proposition few would disagree with, but that males and females are identical, and thus can serve as entirely interchangeable parts in the structure of marriage. This contention is biologically absurd, and "same-sex marriage" is thus an oxymoron.

The fact is that for men, women, and children, the real benefits of marriage accrue to natural marriage. There is no evidence that homosexual unions would produce the same benefits, and considerable evidence that they would do harm. The harm that is done is a big subject, and I devote Chapter Six to it. For now, let's limit our look to the real benefits of natural marriage.

The Real Benefits of Marriage

To this point, I have focused on marriage as a natural institution that serves an important public purpose. But there is another, even more pragmatic reason to support natural marriage. *Society gives benefits to marriage because marriage gives benefits to society.* To summarize it, a massive amount of social science research has shown beyond a shadow of a doubt that married husbands and wives, and their children, are happier, healthier, and more prosperous than people in any other living situation

Let's take a closer look at some of these "benefits of marriage."

- A five-year study released in 1998 found that continuously married people experience better emotional health and less depression than people of any other marital status.[2]
- A 1990 review of research found that married people also have better physical health, while the unmarried have

significantly higher rates of mortality—about 50 percent higher for women and 250 percent higher for men.[3]

- Rates of violent abuse by intimate partners are four times higher among never-married women, and twelve times higher among divorced and separated women, than they are among married women.[4]
- Married people are less likely to be the victims of any type of violent crime than are those who have divorced, separated, or never married.[5]
- Families headed by married couples have much higher incomes and greater financial assets.[6]
- Married couples who are sexually faithful experience more physical pleasure and emotional satisfaction in their sexual relations than do any other sexually active people.[7]

Children raised by married parents, meanwhile, experience lower rates of many social pathologies, including:

- Premarital childbearing[8]
- Illicit drug use[9]
- Arrest[10]
- Health, emotional, or behavioral problems[11]
- Poverty[12]
- School failure or expulsion[13]

These benefits are then passed on to future generations, because children raised by married parents are themselves less likely to cohabit or to divorce as adults.[14]

Britney's Tale:
Do Straight Failures Make Gay Rights?

When conservatives like me say that we are trying to "protect" or "preserve" the institution of marriage by opposing homosexual marriage, one response is common—what is there left to protect? Premarital sex, cohabitation, unwed pregnancies, and single parenthood are already rampant. Divorce rates are approaching 50 percent. Deadbeat dads abandon their kids, and celebrities move in and out of marriages like they change their wardrobes, exemplified by "pop tart" Britney Spears getting married in Las Vegas and having that marriage annulled in the course of fifty-five hours.[15] Meanwhile, the entertainment industry makes a mockery of marriage by turning it into a made-for-TV competition with shows like *The Bachelor* and *Who Wants to Marry a Millionaire?* Haven't heterosexuals done a pretty good job of destroying the "institution of marriage" all by themselves?

There's only one possible answer to this: Yes.

The fifty-five-hour marriage of Britney Spears—to take the most recent, celebrated example—does indeed make a mockery of marriage, and conservative commentators were quick to say so. For example, Tony Perkins, president of the Family Research Council, condemned Spears's behavior both in his daily e-mail, *The Washington Update*, and in a radio commentary. Nevada's lax marriage laws, which require no waiting period to obtain a license, and its lax divorce laws, which have made it a mecca for divorcing couples for decades, should not be emulated by any other state. In fact, the first federal constitutional amendment ever proposed to address the issue of marriage was one endorsed by President Theodore Roosevelt—targeted at the Nevada marriage laws.[16]

Heterosexuals severing the link between marriage and sexual activity, and marriage and childrearing, has done the most damage to the institution of marriage. The severing of these ties has led to sexual promiscuity, an epidemic of sexually transmitted diseases, unwanted pregnancies, abortions, single parenthood, and divorce.

This is why the Family Research Council and other similar groups describe themselves as "pro-family," rather than merely "anti-gay." We are committed to protecting the natural family and preserving its benefits for society against all of these threats—not just the homosexual one. It is primarily because of the dangers of premarital heterosexual sex that we promote abstinence-until-marriage education in our schools. It is to protect the natural fruit of heterosexual unions—children—that we oppose abortion. It is to provide every child with the benefits of a married mother and father that we promote adoption. And it is to preserve the institution of marriage that we favor divorce reform efforts that would roll back "no-fault" divorce and make it harder to dissolve a marriage (efforts such as Louisiana's pioneering "covenant marriage" law, which was sponsored by Family Research Council president Tony Perkins when he was a Louisiana state legislator). It is to encourage more adults to enjoy the economic benefits of marriage that we support President Bush's Healthy Marriage Initiative, which will provide voluntary supports to lower-income people interested in marriage. We are very concerned about the damage to the institution of marriage that has been done by heterosexuals, and we are working hard to implement public policies that will mitigate or undo that damage.

But most of these trends, damaging as they are, have resulted from a slow and steady erosion of the values surrounding marriage in the culture at large. The movement for homosexual marriage, on the other hand, does not represent a slow erosion. Instead, it constitutes a direct, frontal attack on the very definition of the institution of marriage.

Some homosexual activists make the argument that "heterosexuals have already damaged marriage," hoping to generate enough "straight guilt" to disarm arguments about "the sanctity of marriage." They argue that "marriage is too far gone [because of heterosexual failures] to save it." But this is fatalism that we must never accept about the most crucial institution of our society.

Other advocates of homosexual marriage, however, argue that legalizing homosexual marriage would *strengthen* the institution of marriage. They suggest that opening it up to a class of couples that desperately want to participate in it would help reverse the tendency among heterosexuals to take marriage for granted or treat it as unimportant.

I will deal with this argument in more detail in the next chapter with the evidence that the nature of homosexual partnerships is very different from the nature of a typical heterosexual marriage, particularly in the duration of the relationship and the practice (or neglect) of sexual fidelity. This suggests that rather than participating in the institution of marriage as it has historically been understood, homosexuals actually want to reshape marriage in the image of their own relationships.

The "gay rights movement" comes from the "sexual revolution" of the 1960s that promoted "free love," "free" in that it separated elements—sexual relations, childbearing, childrearing, marriage, sexual fidelity, and lifelong commitment—that were once considered an inseparable package. Homosexuals themselves have embraced the free love philosophy wholeheartedly— particularly homosexual men, among whom promiscuity is the rule rather than the exception. At the same time, acceptance within the wider society of the notion that "all sex acts are equal" has been crucial to overcome the natural revulsion of heterosexuals toward the unnatural acts of homosexuals. Only acceptance of the "free love" and "all sex acts are equal" philosophies can bring about widespread acceptance of homosexuality—which is exactly what homosexuals desire most.

Now, homosexual activists believe they have reached the end game in this push for acceptance. Tolerance and compassion are no longer enough—they demand affirmation and celebration of their behavior and relationships. And even that will not satisfy, if they cannot have the official public subsidization and solemnization of those relationships through the institution of civil marriage.

Yet marriage is an institution that is intrinsically at odds with the values of the sexual revolution. It is, as I will show, extremely unlikely that the vast majority of homosexuals will curtail their sexual behavior to conform to the standards of marriage. Instead, the legalization of homosexual marriage would affirm and celebrate the very free love philosophy that is destroying marriage. "Homosexuality" and "marriage" are as fundamentally incompatible as are "free love" and "sexual faithfulness."

Same-Sex Marriage:

WHO NEEDS IT? WHO WANTS IT?

Of course, the key questions in deciding whether homosexual marriage should be legalized deal first with the principles involved. Does prohibiting homosexual marriage violate some principle of "equality" or "justice?" Or does allowing it violate the very order of nature?

The next question has to do with consequences—specifically, whether the legalization of homosexual marriage would, on balance, be helpful to society or harmful to it.

However, there are also factual matters that must be addressed. Would homosexual civil marriage actually make a large difference in the quality of life for most homosexuals? How many people would the legalization of same-sex "marriage" actually affect? Is there actually a large constituency across the country demanding this change in social policy? And what is really driving this agenda?

The "Benefits" Bogeyman

One of the key arguments used in favor of homosexual civil marriage is the claim that homosexual couples are being unjustly denied the "benefits" that are granted to married people under the law. For example, homosexual activist groups make much of the "1,138 benefits" of marriage that have been identified in federal law by the U.S. General Accounting Office. Actually, that list includes any federal law or regulation that even mentions marital status. Thus not all of the 1,138 are actually "benefits, rights, or privileges" at all. Some, in fact, impose additional burdens. Nevertheless, the thought of being "denied over a thousand benefits" makes for a good sound bite.[1]

The Supreme Judicial Court of Massachusetts made a similar claim in its decision ordering homosexual marriage: "The benefits accessible only by way of a marriage license are enormous, touching nearly every aspect of life and death."[2]

There are two possible responses to this. One is to reiterate an important principle: *Society gives benefits to marriage because marriage gives benefits to society*. The burden of proof, therefore, must be on homosexuals to demonstrate that their relationships benefit society in the same way and to the same degree as natural heterosexual marriages, rather than the burden resting on society to demonstrate why homosexuals should be "denied" these benefits. This more proper burden of proof is one that homosexuals cannot meet.

A relevant question, however, is this: Do homosexuals really suffer as gravely as they say from being denied the "benefits of marriage?" I believe the answer is no, for a very simple reason: *Most of the "protections" afforded to married couples under the law are already available to homosexual couples by other means.* Specifically, as noted in Chapter One, most of these protections can be secured through private contractual arrangements that are legal for *any* two adults to make, which do not require marriage.

In fact, the websites of the leading homosexual activist groups contain detailed information on how to make such arrangements, complete with convenient sample legal documents. For example, the Lambda Legal Defense and Education Fund supplies information on:

- Joint tenancy on leases
- Joint ownership of property
- Joint bank accounts
- Durable power of attorney for asset management
- Durable power of attorney for health care (or health care proxy)
- Wills
- Living wills
- Revocable trusts
- Parenting agreements (for homosexual couples who are "co-parenting")
- Conservator, committee, and guardianship appointments
- Funeral arrangements[3]

The Human Rights Campaign includes information on many of the above, adding to the list:

- Domestic partnership agreement
- Sperm donor agreement
- Hospital visitation authorization[4]

Hospital Visitation

The last one in this list is worth special note. A favorite "benefit" that homosexual activists talk about, because it tugs at people's hearts, is the right to visit their partners in the hospital. As these lists show, this is a right that can be legally guaranteed without marriage.[5]

Except when a doctor limits visitation for medical reasons, final authority over who may visit an adult patient rests with that patient. This is and should be the case regardless of the sexual orientation or marital status of the patient or the visitor.

The only situation in which there would be a possibility that the blood relatives of a patient might attempt to exclude the patient's homosexual partner is if the patient is unable to express his or her wishes due to unconsciousness or mental incapacity. Homosexual partners concerned about this (remote) possibility can effectively preclude it by granting to one another a health care proxy (the legal right to make medical decisions for the patient) and a power of attorney (the right to make all legal decisions for another person). Marriage is not necessary for this. It is extraordinarily unlikely that a hospital would exclude someone who holds the health care proxy and power of attorney for a patient from visiting that patient, except for medical reasons.

The hypothetical "hospital visitation hardship" is nothing but an emotional smokescreen to distract people from the more serious implications of radically redefining marriage.

Inheritance

Another frequently cited worry is that homosexuals would not be able to leave their estates to their partners when they die. As with the hospital visitation issue, the concern over inheritance rights is something that simply does not require marriage to resolve it. Nothing in current law prevents homosexual partners from being joint owners of property such as a home or a car, in which case the survivor would automatically become the owner if the partner dies.

An individual may leave his estate to whomever he wishes—again, without regard to sexual orientation or marital status—simply by writing a will. As with the hospital visitation issue, blood relatives would only be able to overrule the surviving homosexual partner in the event that the deceased had failed to record his wishes in a common, inexpensive legal document. Changing the definition of a fundamental social institution like marriage is a rather extreme way of addressing this issue. Preparing a will is a much simpler solution.

Do They Work?

Some homosexual spokesmen might claim that these arrangements are a rather tenuous substitute for marriage, vulnerable to challenge from homophobic officials or relatives at any turn. However, Lambda Legal asks the question, "Will my legal documents giving authority to my lover be recognized by the legal system?"—and answers, "Generally, yes. Any legally competent adult may draft a will, a power of attorney, a living will, a contract..."

As to the fear that the agreements might be challenged, they say, "Should your biological/legally recognized family challenge any of your legal documents, they will have to prove that you were not competent" or that the document "was the result of undue influence, fraud, or duress. None of these challenges is easy for your family to prove." Indeed, they cite only one court

case, in Georgia, in which a lower court struck down a homosexual "domestic partnership contract" because of that state's
sodomy law. However, the Georgia Supreme Court overturned
that decision and the U.S. Supreme Court has since struck
down all sodomy laws.[6]

Homosexual activists argue that many of the protections
such documents offer are granted automatically to couples who
are legally married. While that is true to some extent, it is also
true that many of these documents are recommended even for
couples who are already legally married. In fact, for samples of
the health care proxy and living will, the Human Rights Campaign refers people to the website of a group called "Partnership for Caring"—which includes a prominent picture of a
heterosexual couple on its home page.[7] My wife and I made a
point of going to a lawyer to draw up a last will and testament
after our son was born—and the lawyer threw in a durable
power of attorney and health care proxy form at no extra cost.

Cost, in fact, is another issue that is raised by the advocates
of homosexual marriage. Yet the Human Rights Campaign
admits that the cost of estate planning can be as low as $250.[8]

Social Security

There are, of course, some "benefits" of marriage that are only
available to married people (and will continue to be, even with
the advent of homosexual civil marriage in Massachusetts, due
to the federal Defense of Marriage Act). One of these is the
granting of spousal benefits under the Social Security system.

It is ironic that activists are now seeking Social Security
survivor benefits for homosexual partners, since Congress orig-

inally intended them as a way of supporting a very traditional family structure—one in which the husband worked to provide the family's income while the wife stayed home to keep house and raise the children. Social Security survivor benefits were designed to recognize the non-monetary contribution made to a family by the homemaking and child-rearing activities of a wife and mother, and to ensure that a woman and her children would not become destitute if the man of the house were to die.

The Supreme Court ruled in the 1970s that such benefits must not be limited by the sex of the surviving spouse. Nevertheless, the premise of the benefits is to compensate the homemaker who stays home to raise children.

Far fewer homosexual couples than heterosexual ones are raising children at all. Very few homosexual couples have a "traditional" division of labor and roles. They are far more likely to consist of two wage earners, each of whom can be supported in old age by their own personal Social Security pension.

Survivor benefits for the legal (biological or adopted) *children* of homosexual parents (as opposed to their partners) are already available under current law, so "marriage" rights for homosexual couples are unnecessary to protect the interests of these children.[9]

How Many Homosexuals Would "Marry?"

In addition to the question of how much homosexuals actually need legal marriage, there is a serious question as to just how many homosexuals might take advantage of this newfound "right."

In popular media, the figure most often cited for the size of the homosexual population in America is 10 percent. For example, a web search for the words "10 percent gay" returned 124,000 hits, including: a gay-oriented shopping site for "10% Productions;"[10] numerous homosexual student groups on college campuses called the "Ten-Percent Society;"[11] *tenpercentbent*, described as "the e-zine for glbt [gay, lesbian, bisexual, transgender] youth;"[12] and the "Ten Percent Revue," an off-Broadway musical described as a "celebration of gay life."[13] Groups promoting a pro-homosexual agenda in schools endorse books titled *One Teenager in Ten: Writings by Gay and Lesbian Youth*, a sequel titled *Two Teenagers in Twenty*, and another book called *One Teacher in Ten: Gay and Lesbian Educators Tell Their Stories*.[14]

Yet no scientific, population-based survey has ever shown that anywhere close to 10 percent of American adults identify themselves as homosexual or bisexual. And now, in a remarkable and little-noticed statement, a coalition of leading pro-homosexual activist groups has admitted in a legal brief that only "2.8 percent of the male, and 1.4 percent of the female, population identify themselves as gay, lesbian, or bisexual."[15]

The admission that the actual size of the homosexual or bisexual population is far smaller than the 10 percent myth would suggest came in an amicus curiae (or "friend of the court") brief filed with the U.S. Supreme Court in the case of *Lawrence v. Texas*. The brief was filed by a coalition of thirty-one pro-homosexual activist groups, including some of the leading national organizations such as the Human Rights Campaign; the National Gay and Lesbian Task Force; Parents, Families and Friends of Lesbians and Gays; the Gay & Lesbian

Alliance Against Defamation; and the People For the American Way Foundation.

The unusually candid statement about the relatively low number of homosexuals in the population appeared on page sixteen of the brief. The text contains the assertion: "There are approximately six million openly gay men and women in the United States, and 450,000 gay men and lesbians in Texas."[16] After the national figure there appears a citation, number 42 in the brief. The note at the bottom of the page reads as follows (in its entirety):

> The most widely accepted study of sexual practices in the United States is the National Health and Social Life Survey (NHSLS). The NHSLS found that 2.8 percent of the male, and 1.4 percent of the female, population identify themselves as gay, lesbian, or bisexual. *See* Laumann, et al., *The Social Organization of Sex: Sexual Practices in the United States* (1994). This amounts to nearly 4 million openly gay men and 2 million women who identify as lesbian.[17]

Unfortunately, despite their candor about the small percentage of the population that is homosexual, the authors of the brief still managed to overestimate the actual number of "openly gay men and women" by more than a third. That's because the figures of "4 million openly gay men and 2 million women who identify as lesbian" were apparently arrived at by multiplying the 2.8 percent and 1.4 percent figures by the total number of males and females in the U.S. population. Yet it hardly seems reasonable to count any of the sixty million

Americans who are fourteen years old or younger (and particularly the forty million who are nine or younger) as "openly gay men and women."[18]

If one applies the percentage figures from the NHSLS instead to only the population of men and women eighteen years old or older, one arrives at an estimate that perhaps 4.3 million Americans (2.8 million men and 1.5 million women) identify themselves as homosexual or bisexual.[19] It is important as well to note that the "bisexual" component in that is fairly high. In fact, the percentage of the population that identifies themselves exclusively as homosexual (not bisexual) is only 2 percent for men and 0.9 percent for women, or about two million men and slightly less than one million women.[20] And even an exclusive homosexual self-identification is not always matched by similarly exclusive behavior. The NHSLS found that only 0.9 percent of men and 0.4 percent of women reported having only same-sex sexual partners since age eighteen, a figure that would represent a total of only about 1.4 million Americans (men and women combined).[21]

In fact, the book on the NHSLS that was cited in the homosexual groups' brief refers as well to "the myth of 10 percent," noting that it was probably drawn from part of the research of Alfred Kinsey.[22] However, even Kinsey actually concluded that only "4 percent of the white males are exclusively homosexual throughout their lives."[23] And the book by Laumann notes that Kinsey used research methods that "would all tend to bias Kinsey's results toward higher estimates of homosexuality (and other rarer sexual practices) than those he would have obtained using probability sampling."[24]

The Laumann book also mentions in a footnote that "Bruce Voeller (1990) claims to have originated the 10 percent estimate as part of the modern gay rights movement's campaign in the late 1970s to convince politicians and the public that 'We [gays and lesbians] Are Everywhere.' At the time, Voeller was the chair of the National Gay Task Force"—forerunner of the National Gay and Lesbian Task Force, which was represented by the recent brief.[25]

While the number of people who identify themselves as homosexual or bisexual is quite low, the number of self-identified homosexuals who are actually cohabiting in some sort of long-term homosexual "partnership" is far lower. Although the U.S. Census does not inquire as to people's sexual orientation, the 2000 census for the first time gave people who are not married the option of declaring themselves to be "unmarried partners." Although the vast majority of "unmarried partners" are cohabiting heterosexuals, by identifying persons who declared themselves to be the "unmarried partner" of a principal householder of the same sex, we can infer fairly precisely how many cohabiting homosexual couples there are, both nationally and at the state and local level.

The 2000 census identified 301,026 male "unmarried partner" households nationwide, as well as 293,365 female "unmarried partner" households. This adds up to a total of 594,391 households in America headed by homosexual couples. However, this total represents only 0.99 percent of the "coupled" households in America (coupled households are those headed by an opposite-sex married couple, an opposite-sex cohabiting couple, or a same-sex cohabiting couple). In other words, heterosexual couples outnumber homosexual ones by a margin of 100 to 1. Viewed in relation to the total population, including those not in any coupled relationship, we find that only 0.57 percent of Americans over age eighteen, or about one in every 175, is living in a homosexual partnership.[26]

I studied what this might mean for the population in Massachusetts, the first state to legally recognize homosexual "marriages." In Massachusetts, the percentage of households headed by same-sex couples is somewhat higher than the national average. However, such households still represent only 1.29 percent of all coupled households. The census reports 7,943 male "unmarried partner" households, and 9,156 female "unmarried partner" households, for a total of 17,099.[27] The individuals in those same-sex couples represent only one out of 142 adult residents of the Commonwealth.[28]

However, there is reason to doubt whether a majority of those same-sex couples would marry even if permitted to do so. In 2000, the state of Vermont, on the basis of a ruling by that state's supreme court, became the first in the nation to extend virtually all of the legal benefits of marriage to same-sex couples by virtue of the "civil union." Yet a study of the impact of civil unions, conducted by University of Vermont psychologist Esther Rothblum and reported in *USA Today*, found that only 936 of the 1,933 same-sex couples in Vermont (48 percent) have actually entered into a civil union.[29] This situation, in which fewer than half of the same-sex cohabiting couples have even sought legal recognition of their relationship, is in stark contrast to the situation among opposite-sex couples—where married-couple households exceed "unmarried-partner" households by a ratio of 7 to 1.[30]

If the same ratio were to hold true in Massachusetts, it would suggest that about 8,280 same-sex couples in Massachusetts might be expected to seek the formal legal status of "marriage"— a group that represents only one in every 293 adults in the state.

Of course, if the claims of homosexual couples to a moral or legal "right" to marry were justified in principle, it would not matter how many of them there are. Nevertheless, it is startling that Massachusetts has undertaken such a radical step as changing the essential definition of our most basic social institution merely to satisfy the personal desires of such a tiny proportion of the population.

Who Wants Same-Sex Marriage?

In a democracy, public opinion ought to have something to do with the making of public policy. Therefore, it's appropriate to ask how much political support there is for changing the definition of marriage, and where it comes from. There are two key points to make on this score.

The American public doesn't want homosexual marriage

It's clear that the agenda for homosexual marriage now being foisted upon America by an elite corps of judges is totally contrary to the will of the American people. Poll after poll has now demonstrated this. That opposition has only grown since the U.S. Supreme Court declared homosexual sodomy to be a constitutional right in June 2003 and the Supreme Judicial Court of Massachusetts ruled that natural marriage had no "rational basis" in November 2003.

A Gallup poll, for instance, showed that opposition to homosexual marriage jumped ten points between June and December 2003, from 55 percent to 65 percent. An NBC/*Wall Street Journal* poll showed a similar jump, from 51 percent in July 2003 to 62 percent in March 2004. A PSRA/Pew poll showed that the percentage who "oppose" or "strongly oppose" legalizing homosexual marriage went up from 53 percent to 63 percent between summer 2003 and February 2004. A FOX News/Opinion Dynamics poll taken immediately after the *Goodridge* decision in November 2003 showed 66 percent opposing same-sex marriage with only 25 percent supporting it.

And although homosexual activists boast of the increasing acceptance of homosexuality, a PSRA/*Newsweek* poll showed that opposition to legal gay marriage is just as high in 2004 as it was twelve years earlier, at 58 percent. In fact, what is truly shocking is that America is being asked to put its highest stamp of approval, civil marriage, on relationships that are not only *not* viewed as marriages, but are considered "morally wrong" by a majority of Americans in every poll that has ever asked the question.

In light of this clear public position, it is quite puzzling that so few politicians seem willing to take a clear stand in defense of natural marriage. It is even more puzzling when the intensity of people's feelings is taken into account. For example, a 2003 NAES poll showed that 49 percent of Americans strongly oppose same-sex marriage, while only 17 percent strongly favor it. A Gallup/CNN/*USA Today* poll in September 2003 found that 48 percent of Americans believe same-sex marriage would "change our society for the worse," while only 10 percent think it would change society for the better. A presidential candidate who favors gay marriage would be more likely to get the votes of only 10 percent of the populace, and less likely to win 49 percent.[31]

The polling numbers specifically on a federal constitutional amendment to define marriage as the union of one man and one woman are somewhat more mixed. However, this appears to largely reflect confusion about different proposed versions of an amendment and how they might treat "civil unions" that grant the benefits of marriage without the name. According to The Polling Company, 67 percent of the public favors some form of a federal marriage amendment that would define civil marriage as the union of one man and one woman, while only 26 percent of the public opposes the idea altogether.[32]

On any other issue with poll numbers like that, politicians would be falling all over each other trying to get on the right side. One must assume that the overwhelming media bias in favor of the homosexual agenda, and the charges of "bigotry" and "hatred" inevitably thrown at anyone who challenges it, have simply cowed too many of our public officials.

Many homosexuals are opposed to same-sex "marriage"

For example, James T. Sears, a gay historian, has written that fifty years ago, the nation's first major gay magazine, *One*, featured a cover with the question: "Homosexual Marriage?" And yet, according to Sears, the author actually "disparaged the prospect of state-sanctioned homosexual unions." The author of the story declared that the Mattachine Society (an early homosexual rights organization) "desires to win from society acceptance for the deviate." He celebrated the fact that homosexuals are "permitted promiscuity" while "heterosexuals...must be married to enjoy sexual intercourse." And he worried that marriage would lead homosexuals to follow the heterosexual model: "No more sexual abandon: imagine!" Sears himself shares the concern, lamenting that today's gay leaders "have entered a Faustian bargain trading equal rights with heterosexuals in lieu of sexual liberation for all. We...advance reform devoid of desire. We march for equal rights, not the right to f[**]k."[33]

Suzanna Walters, a Georgetown University professor, supports the right to homosexual marriage as a legal matter, but says that "whether gays should want to be part of that institution is another matter," noting that "a robust debate has raged in the gay community." Walters points out, for instance, "Feminists have argued for years that marriage is a troubled and troubling institution...built on the ownership of women and children [and] sexual and emotional violence." She reminds gay activists that "reimagining love, sex and family was at the heart of the liberationist ideal," while decrying "the fiction of the connubial couple, blissfully enthralled and wholly fulfilled, sanctioned by the state and protected by the white picket fences of family and faith." She concludes that the push for homosexual marriage is "a disheartening sign of the distance from our liberationist past."[34]

Similar sentiments have been expressed in other countries wrestling with the homosexual marriage question. Paul Flynn, a thirty-two-year-old homosexual writing in the British newspaper *The Guardian*, reported that "the thought of a priest pronouncing the couple in front of me husband and husband makes me feel icky." In response to anticipated "torrents of abuse from gay inclusionists," Flynn notes,

> I've been to a couple of parties celebrating gay love that were sweet and jolly in equal measure. But neither dressed up the occasion as marriage. Both seemed implicitly to understand that a gay partnership might be equal to a straight one but that doesn't necessarily make it the same. . . . Marriage is about men and women."[35]

Even in the first place in North America to legalize homosexual marriage—the Canadian province of Ontario—some homosexuals are skeptical of marriage. A front-page article in the *New York Times* on August 31, 2003, reported that in the first two and a half months after Ontario's highest court legalized "marriage" for same-sex couples, fewer than five hundred same-sex Canadian couples had taken out marriage licenses in Toronto, even though the city has over six thousand such couples registered as permanent partners.

The *Times* reported that "skepticism about marriage is a recurring refrain among Canadian gay couples," noting that "many gays express the fear that it will undermine their notions of who they are. They say they want to maintain the unique aspects of their culture and their place at the edge of social change." Mitchel Raphael, the editor of *fab*, a Toronto gay magazine, said, "I'd be for marriage if I thought gay people would challenge and change the institution and not buy into the traditional meaning of 'till death do us part' and monogamy forever." And Rinaldo

Walcott, a sociologist at the University of Tornoto, lamented, "Will queers now have to live with the heterosexual forms of guilt associated with something called cheating?"[36]

In fact, a poll by Raphael's magazine found that a majority of homosexuals in Canada are actually opposed to same-sex marriage. Only 36 percent of respondents in the *fab* magazine poll believe that homosexuals should "settle for marriage and nothing less." Raphael wrote in the Toronto *Globe and Mail*, "Fear exists in the gay community that marriage will be used as a means to clean up its overt, institutionalized sex culture"—one that lacks the "baggage of eternal monogamy."[37]

The Real Agenda: The Affirmation, not the Institution

This chapter has demonstrated that the tangible "benefits" to homosexuals from civil marriage would be relatively small; that there are relatively few homosexuals who are likely to marry; and that homosexuals have little interest in participating in the institution of marriage as it has historically been understood. It leads one to wonder why such an intense push is now underway to achieve the legalization of homosexual marriage.

The logical answer would seem to be that this campaign is not really about marriage at all. Instead, it is about the desperate desire of homosexuals for society at large to affirm that homosexuality (not just homosexual individuals, but homosexual sex acts) is the full equivalent of heterosexuality in every way—morally, socially, and legally.

Some homosexuals have said as much. In an editorial in the *Washington Blade*, a gay newspaper, one writer said, "This is about more than that little certified piece of paper, or even all the legal benefits it brings. It's about the recognition that our love is as valid, just as real, just as much worth celebrating as anyone else's."[38] And Andrew Sullivan, an early and vocal advocate of homosexual marriage, wrote in *Time* magazine that he is motivated by the thought of a "young kid" who is gay. "I want him to know that his love has dignity, that he does indeed have a future as a full and equal part of the human race. Only marriage will do that."[39]

What a strange argument this is—that we should demolish the definition of our most basic social institution for no other reason than to boost the sagging self-esteem of a troubled few.

6

What Harm Would It Do?

One of the key questions raised by homosexual activists is this: "What harm could it possibly do to *your* heterosexual marriage if the homosexual couple down the street gets married?" The question is usually posed in a mocking way, as if it is obvious that there could be no harm at all. Are heterosexual couples going to suddenly be rushing into divorce court the day after homosexual marriage becomes legal?

But the question is not what harm homosexual marriage would do to a particular heterosexual couple. The proper question is whether homosexual marriage would harm society as a whole and in the long run. The fact is, there are a number of harms that we can expect society to incur if homosexual marriage is legalized. Let's examine them now.

The Bishop Robinson Effect

To believe that homosexual marriage would not harm heterosexual marriage, one would have to believe that no one who is
in a heterosexual marriage could ever be tempted by the possibility of a homosexual relationship—and we know that that is
not the case. Whenever I hear people say "homosexuals are not
allowed to marry," I wonder why the press doesn't point out
that many, many "homosexuals" (that is, people who currently
identify themselves as gay or lesbian) have already been married. And they have been married legally, under civil law, with
all the rights and benefits of marriage—because they have been
married to a person of the opposite sex.

One prominent example of this is Eugene Robinson, the
homosexual man who was elected a bishop of the Episcopal
Church in New Hampshire. The press covered the controversy
over whether an active homosexual who lives with a same-sex
partner should be chosen as a leader of the church. Less attention, unfortunately, was paid to the fact that Bishop Robinson
had previously been married to a woman for fifteen years and
had functioned successfully enough as a heterosexual to have
fathered two children. Robinson and his wife agreed to divorce
in 1987 when their daughters were eight and five.[1] The Robin-
sons even created a bizarre church ceremony (not found in the
Book of Common Prayer), in which they returned their wedding rings to symbolically release each other from their wedding vows.[2] Robinson met his current homosexual partner
shortly after his divorce.[3]

A study of the same-sex couples who live in Vermont and
have entered into civil unions in that state showed that an aston-

ishing 40 percent of them had previously been married. Whether this means that 40 percent of the individuals had been married or that 40 percent of the couples included at least one partner who had previously been married is unclear. But even if it is the latter (meaning that at least 20 percent of the individuals had been married), it is still an amazingly high number considering the supposed "immutability" of homosexuality. Another piece of evidence reinforcing the high rates of previous marriages among homosexuals comes from studies of homosexual parenting. Although profiles of homosexual parents usually dwell on the subject of adoption, many children raised by homosexuals are not adopted, but were conceived in previous heterosexual relationships or marriages the homosexual parents had.[4]

If Bishop Robinson—and of course others like him—divorced his wife and later found and moved in with a homosexual lover, will not the legalization of homosexual marriage really make such abandonments more likely in the future by removing some of the social stigmas attached to them?

We can learn an important lesson from our experience with no-fault divorce. While the temptation to adultery and divorce has always existed, it is a fact that after the passage of no-fault divorce laws, the divorce rate jumped dramatically. Researchers have found that no-fault divorce led to an increase in divorce rates in forty-four states,[5] possibly by as much as 25 percent.[6] Similarly, changing the legal definition of marriage will likely reduce the social stigma against homosexuality and increase the number of married people who would endanger their marriage by actively pursuing a homosexual relationship.

To the question "What straight person would want to be married to a homosexual anyway?" one could just as easily ask,

"Who would want to remain married to an adulterer?" The answer is that many spouses would rather save their marriage—especially if children are involved—rather than see the other spouse pursue a no-fault divorce and pursue homosexual inclinations. And it is in the interest of their children and of society that such marriages be saved.

I once made this argument in a public forum, and an audience member challenged it by spinning out a long, hypothetical story about a married person who becomes aware of his homosexual inclinations, and shares with his understanding spouse that he cannot remain in their heterosexual marriage any longer without being "dishonest" to who he really is. My response to this elaborate scenario was simple—I would never call it "dishonest" for a person to fulfill the vows he made at his wedding. The notion that an individual is morally entitled to dump his spouse because of a new sexual attraction is itself one of the gravest threats to marriage today. This leads to another point.

Homosexuals Will Change Marriage More than Marriage Will Change Homosexuals

One of the greatest fallacies being promulgated by the homosexual activists is the idea that homosexual couples are exactly like heterosexual couples, except for the sex of their chosen partner. Therefore, the argument goes, once they are granted the same access to the rights of civil marriage that opposite-sex couples have, we should be able to expect their "marriages" to be approximately the same in character as opposite-sex ones. There are several key facts that contradict this argument.

Homosexuals are less likely to enter into long-term relationships at all

Despite major changes in cultural attitudes and behavior in the last several generations, marriage remains normative for heterosexuals. The vast majority of heterosexuals are currently married, have been married, or will marry in the course of their lifetime. This is true despite the increased availability of sex outside of marriage (including couples living together). In other words, most heterosexuals still see finding a lifelong mate and making a legally binding commitment to that person in marriage as a key life goal.

Yet, according to the 2000 census, which for the first time gave us hard statistics on the number of cohabiting homosexual couples nationwide, only 1.2 million homosexuals out of an estimated 4.3 million homosexual or bisexual adults live as couples—far smaller than the percentage of heterosexual adults who are married (even excluding heterosexuals who are cohabiting outside of marriage). And, as we have seen, fewer than half of the homosexual Vermont couples identified by the census have even bothered to enter into a civil union, since such unions became legal in Vermont. This is in sharp contrast with the situation among heterosexuals, where married couples outnumber cohabiting ones by a ratio of 7 to 1.

More interesting data comes from anthropologist and columnist Stanley Kurtz. He has demonstrated that giving the full legal rights of marriage to homosexual couples in Sweden and Norway (through what are essentially "civil unions") has actually accelerated a cultural trend away from marriage. In other words, not only are homosexuals less likely to enter into a legally binding commitment to one another than are heterosexuals, but since such unions were legalized, heterosexuals have become less likely to marry than they were before. Perhaps most alarmingly, Kurtz has found that this wholesale retreat from marriage has come even among couples who have children—suggesting that the trend will result in even more children (and not just those with homosexual parents) growing up without the stability of having a married mother and father. "Once in place, gay marriage symbolically ratified the separation of marriage and parenthood," Kurtz explains. He continues:

> If, as in Norway, gay marriage were imposed here by a socially liberal cultural elite, it would likely speed us on the way toward the classic Nordic pattern of less frequent marriage, more frequent out-of-wedlock birth, and skyrocketing family dissolution. In the American context, this would be a disaster.[7]

I have heard many homosexual activists argue that homosexual couples ought to be allowed to marry; but I have never heard a homosexual activist say that if such marriages are legalized, homosexuals ought to marry, as opposed to having sex or cohabiting without the benefit of marriage. Homosexual marriage ultimately would constitute official public and social endorsement of the entire homosexual lifestyle—including the right not to marry, even if one is sexually active and even if one has children. Of course, everyone, including heterosexuals, already has such a right as a legal matter. But the increased exercise of such choices on the part of homosexuals even after gaining a legal "right" to marry would undoubtedly have the cultural effect of making such choices increasingly acceptable among heterosexuals as well. Sexual relations before marriage have already devastated our society by leading to an epidemic of sexually transmitted diseases (which are even more common among homosexuals). Childrearing outside of marriage has already hurt millions of children. Ironically, expanding the legal definition of marriage to include homosexual couples is likely not to strengthen marriage, as the "conservative" advocates of homosexual marriage argue, but to further weaken it by accelerating a societal retreat from marriage altogether.

"Conservative" advocates of homosexual marriage would have more credibility if they were to join social conservatives in calling for chastity outside of marriage. That, however, is one thing I have never heard from a homosexual activist. In fact, many homosexuals expressly renounce such a notion.

We can with some confidence predict that if homosexual marriage is legalized, the percentage of homosexuals who choose to marry will always be lower than the percentage of heterosexuals who choose to marry, and the percentage of heterosexuals who choose to marry will also decline—with negative consequences for society.

Homosexuals are less likely to be sexually faithful to each other, even in the context of a "long-term partnership"

One value that remains remarkably strong, even among people who have multiple sexual partners before marriage, is the belief that marriage itself is a sexually exclusive relationship. Among married heterosexuals, having sexual relations with anyone other than one's spouse is still considered a grave breach of trust and violation of the marriage covenant by the vast majority of people.

Yet the same cannot be said of homosexuals—particularly of homosexual men. Numerous studies of homosexual relationships, including "partnered" relationships covering a span of decades, have shown that sex with multiple partners is tolerated and often expected, even when one has a "long-term" partner. Perhaps the most startling such study was published in the journal *AIDS*. In the context of studying HIV risk behavior among young homosexual men in the Netherlands (coincidentally, the first country in the world to legalize homosexual civil marriage), the researchers found that homosexual men who were in partnered relationships had an average of eight sexual partners per year outside of the primary relationship.[8] (It must be conceded that having such a partnership did have some "taming" effect upon such men—those without a "permanent" partner had an average of twenty-two sexual partners per year). This is an astonishing contrast to the typical behavior of married heterosexuals, among whom 75 percent of the men and 85 percent of the women report never having had extramarital sex.[9]

Rather than marriage changing the behavior of homosexuals to match the relative sexual fidelity of heterosexuals, it seems likely that the opposite would occur. If homosexual relationships, promiscuity and all, are held up to society as being a fully equal part of the social ideal that is called "marriage," then the value of sexual fidelity as an expected standard of behavior for married people will further erode.

Thus, we can predict that if homosexual marriage is legalized, the percentage of homosexuals who have a faithful, sexually exclusive relationship will always be lower than the percentage of heterosexuals who have such a relationship, but the percentage of married heterosexuals who remain sexually faithful to their spouses will also decline—with negative consequences for society.

Homosexual relationships are much less likely to last a lifetime than are heterosexual marriages

Once again, abundant research has borne out this point. Indeed, the Dutch study mentioned above, which highlighted so dramatically the promiscuous nature of male homosexual relationships, also showed their transience as well. It found that the average male homosexual partnership lasts only one and a half years. In contrast, more than 50 percent of heterosexual marriages last fifteen years or longer.[10]

Older studies came to similar conclusions. In one study of 156 male couples, for instance, only seven had been together for longer than five years (and none of those seven had remained sexually faithful to each other).[11] And a recent study of same-sex divorce in Sweden showed, to the surprise of some, that lesbian couples were even more likely to divorce than were homosexual men, although both divorced at rates higher than heterosexual couples.[12]

How would this affect heterosexual couples? The unstable nature of homosexual partnerships would become part of the accepted norm of marriage. Therefore, we can predict that if homosexual marriage is legalized, the percentage of homosexual couples that remain together for a lifetime will always be lower than the percentage of heterosexual couples that do so, but the percentage of heterosexual couples demonstrating

lifelong commitment will also decline—with negative consequences for society.

"For the Sake of the Kids"

The greatest tragedy resulting from the legalization of homosexual marriage would not be its effect on adults, but its effect
on children. For the first time in history, society would be plac-
ing its highest stamp of official government approval on the
deliberate creation of *permanently* motherless or fatherless
households for children.

Homosexual activists say that having both a mother and a
father simply doesn't matter—having two loving parents is what
counts. But social science research simply does not support this
claim. Dr. Kyle Pruett of Yale Medical School, for example, has
demonstrated in his book *Fatherneed* that fathers contribute to
parenting in ways that mothers do not.[13] On the other hand, Dr.
Brenda Hunter has documented the unique contributions that
mothers make in her book, *The Power of Mother Love*.[14]

Some homosexual couples are deliberately *creating* new children in order to raise them motherless or fatherless from birth.
It is quite striking to read, for example, the model "Donor
Agreement" for sperm donors offered on the Human Rights
Campaign website, and to see the lengths to which they will go
to legally insure that the actual biological father of a child for
a lesbian mother plays no role in the life of the child.[15]

Some homosexual couples who have adopted children claim
that they are providing a better home for children than the
alternatives, such as foster care. But the high rates of sexual
promiscuity, sexually transmitted diseases, mental illness, sub-

stance abuse, and domestic violence among homosexuals cast grave doubt on the stability and suitability of homosexual-headed households for children.

A more specific concern is raised by the data showing that homosexual men are proportionally far more likely to engage in child sexual abuse than are heterosexual men. Though heterosexual men outnumber homosexual men by at least twenty to one, homosexual pedophiles commit about one-third of the total number of child sex offenses.[16] Moreover, a study of convicted child molesters found that 86 percent of offenders against males described themselves as homosexual or bisexual.[17]

Most research on "homosexual parents" thus far that has tried to prove there are no differences between them and heterosexual parents has been marred by serious methodological problems.[18] Even pro-homosexual sociologists Judith Stacey and Timothy Biblarz report that the actual data we have from key studies show the "no differences" claim to be false.

Surveying the research (primarily regarding lesbians) in an *American Sociological Review* article in 2001, Stacey and Biblarz found that:

- Children of lesbians are more likely to engage in homosexual behavior
- Daughters of lesbians are "more sexually adventurous and less chaste"
- Lesbian "co-parent relationships" are more likely to break up than heterosexual marriages[19]

A 1996 study by an Australian sociologist compared children raised by heterosexual married couples, heterosexual cohabiting couples, and homosexual cohabiting couples. It found that the children of heterosexual married couples did the best, and children of homosexual couples the worst, in nine of the thirteen academic and social categories measured.[20]

While the media are all too happy to present rosy pictures of "gay families," the darker side is rarely exposed. Yet the testimonies of adults who were actually raised by homosexuals can be chilling. Kyneret Hope, age twenty-five, writes:

> I experienced [lesbian] separatism as a constant level of anger and negativity. . . . Men were called mutants, straight women were considered disowned sisters who wasted woman-energy on men, and other lesbians were sometimes accused of being government spies.[21]

Michael, age twenty-seven, reports:

> Until I was sixteen or so, I was sexually abused by many straight men [sic], "friends" of my mother's whom I was occasionally left with. . . . Lesbians who hate or fear men take this out on boy children. I suspect that the same thing might happen with gay fathers and girl children.[22]

Kathlean Hill, age twenty, writes:

> I just remember thinking that all lesbians felt the same way my mother felt about everything. If that were true, then all lesbians would talk about men as crude, destructive, dishonest, sleazy creatures that were really not supposed to exist. . . . I decided

that lesbians were a bunch of hypocritical women. Just a bunch of women who preach freedom and individuality, yet their values and beliefs were basically homogeneous. So, at a very young age, lesbianism looked like a bleak future to me. Terre called my sister and me "baby dykes," making us wear these small hand-crafted lesbian signs she had made for us by a local lesbian jeweler. Both my sister, Maureen, and I have always been extremely resentful of that.[23]

Carey Conley, age twenty-one, says:

I was angry that I was not part of a "normal" family and could not live with a "normal" mother. I wondered what I did to deserve this. Why did my biological mother let a lesbian adopt me? How could she think that this life was better than what she could have given me?[24]

Jakii Edwards has written an entire book about being raised by a lesbian home. She summarizes the lessons she learned:

We constantly wonder if we will eventually become gay. There is humiliation when other kids see our parents kissing a same-sex lover in front of us. Trust me, it's hard on the children, no matter how much they love their gay parent. The homosexual community may never admit it, but the damage stemming from their actions can be profound.[25]

If we tolerate the legalization of homosexual marriage, then we as a society will be complicit in that damage.

Downhill Racing: The Slippery Slope

In most of the debate over homosexual marriage, there are arguments and counter-arguments, charges and counter-charges, thrusts and parries. However, there is one argument against homosexual marriage to which its supporters simply have no answer. Their response, instead, is either to stomp their feet and cry foul, or simply to descend into incoherence.

That is the classic "slippery slope" argument—the insight that applying the principle behind legalization of homosexual marriage would inevitably lead to legalization of other sexual deviations and relationships, such as polygamy, incest, or pedophilia.

The "crying foul" response was demonstrated by the reaction to comments made by Senator Rick Santorum, a Republican from Pennsylvania. On April 7, 2003, Santorum gave an interview to Associated Press reporter Lara Jakes Jordan. Anticipating the ruling from the U.S. Supreme Court on the constitutionality of sodomy laws two months later, Santorum warned of the consequences if sodomy was legalized:

> If the Supreme Court says that you have the right to consensual sex within your home, then you have the right to bigamy, you have the right to polygamy, you have the right to incest, you have the right to adultery. You have the right to anything. Does that undermine the fabric of our society? I would argue yes, it does.[26]

Santorum was immediately subjected to a firestorm of criticism from the media and homosexual activists. His remarks were compared to Senator Trent Lott's praise of Strom Thur-mond's segregationist presidential campaign. The Human Rights Campaign called them "deeply discriminatory and insensitive."[27] Columnist Ellen Goodman warned of "the Republican theocracy."[28] One blogger wrote that "the senator is a vacuous boob prone to outrageous gaffs [sic] and crude outbursts of unvarnished bigotry."[29]

What no one was able to do was explain in what way, if any, he was mistaken.

In fact, most of these critics failed to even understand his point. In saying that Santorum "equated homosexuality with incest, bigamy, and polygamy,"[30] they were, quite simply, wrong. He was not attempting to "equate" these behaviors on a moral level at all. He was, instead, pointing out that the *principles* under which people were arguing for the legalization of sodomy would lead, if followed to their logical conclusion, to the legalization of these other behaviors.

If the governing principle that compels the legalization of homosexual sodomy is that "the government has no right to interfere with sexual relationships between consenting adults," then one would *have* to conclude that "the government has no right to interfere with sexual relationships between consenting adults" that are bigamous, polygamous, incestuous, or adulter-ous, either. While there may be a distinction in terms of the average person's visceral reaction to these respective behaviors, there is *no* distinction to be made on any basis that is logical and not purely arbitrary.

The same can be said of marriage. If the natural sexual com-plementarity of male and female and the theoretical procreative capacity of an opposite-sex union are to be discarded as principles central to the definition of marriage, then what is left? According to the arguments of the homosexual marriage advocates, only love and companionship are truly necessary elements of marriage.

But if that is the case, then why should *other* relationships that provide love, companionship, and a lifelong commitment not *also* be recognized as "marriages"—including relationships between adults and children, or between blood relatives, or between three or more adults? And if it violates the equal protection of the laws to deny homosexuals their first choice of marital partner, why would it not do the same to deny pedophiles, polygamists, or the incestuous the right to marry the person (or persons) of their choice?

I had the opportunity to pose this question in a face-to-face debate with Andrew Sullivan, the most prominent "conservative" advocate of homosexual marriage. His response was three-fold:

1. "Marriage in our culture has always been between two persons." (To which I laughed, saying, "That's our argument— 'We've always done it that way.'")
2. "Legalizing polygamy would cause a great deal of social disruption."
3. "Under a system of polygamy, you would have children who wouldn't know who their real parents are."

I could only laugh again and say, "Andrew, you've just named all of *our* arguments against same-sex marriage."[31]

If the slope is slippery enough, the deconstruction of marriage could lead to some unions that are truly absurd—but, amazingly, not without precedent somewhere. For example, Reuters has reported, "A 25-year-old Indian man has married his 80-year-old grandmother because he wanted to take care of her. (Local officials did say such a marriage, which took place in a Hindu temple, is illegal, 'but they have no plans to take action against the couple.')" The same article, meanwhile, said, "Last June, a nine-year-old Indian girl was married to a dog (because 'a priest told her parents the wedding would ward off evil')."[32] Meanwhile in France, "A 35-year-old Frenchwoman became both bride and widow when she married her dead boyfriend." And this one *was* legal—in fact, it required the approval of the French president.[33]

In the more speculative realm, we have a verbatim press release that was reprinted by the *Washington Post*:

> The legalization of same-sex marriages may prepare the way for even more radical unions in the future, according to Canadian professor Stephen Bertman. Bertman foresees the possibility of marriage between humans and their household pets or even inanimate objects such as a beloved car or computer. . . . Bertman offers his views on the evolution of matrimony in the March-April 2004 issue of *The Futurist* magazine.[34]

And let's not forget that the 2004 Pulitzer Prize for Drama went to a play about an East German transvestite titled "I Am My Own Wife."[35]

But the road to polygamy seems the best paved—and the most difficult for homosexual marriage advocates to respond to.

If, as they claim, it is arbitrary and unjust to limit the *sex* of one's marital partner, it is hard to explain why it would not be equally arbitrary and unjust to limit the *number* of marital partners.

It is also hard for them to address for two other reasons. The first is that there is far more precedent cross-culturally for polygamy as an accepted marital structure than there is for homosexual marriage. And the second is that there is a genuine movement for polygamy or "polyamory" in some circles.

The *San Francisco Chronicle* ran a feature on the "polyamory" movement in 2003. The article even quoted Jasmine Walston, the president of "Unitarian Universalists for Polyamory Awareness," as saying, "We're where the gay rights movement was 30 years ago." The story also quoted Barb Greve, a program associate with the Association of Unitarian Universalists' Office of Bisexual, Gay, Lesbian and Transgender Concerns in Boston. Greve, helpfully described as "a transgender person who likes to be called 'he,'" said, "There are people who want to be in committed relationships—whether it's heterosexual marriage, same-sex marriage or polyamory—and that should be acknowledged religiously and legally."[36]

The *Washington Blade* has also featured this topic in a full-page article under the headline "Polygamy advocates buoyed by gay court wins." It quotes Art Spitzer of the American Civil Liberties Union acknowledging, "Yes, I think [*Lawrence v. Texas*] would give a lawyer a foothold to argue such a case. The general framework of that case, that states can't make it a crime to engage in private consensual intimate relationships, is a strong argument."[37]

This argument is already being pressed in the courts. Two convicted bigamists in Utah, Tom Green and Rodney Holm, have appealed to have their convictions overturned—citing the Supreme Court's decision in the sodomy case as precedent (so Senator Santorum was right). And another attorney has filed suit challenging the refusal of the Salt Lake Country clerk to grant a marriage license for G. Lee Cook to take a second wife.[38]

Make no mistake about it—if homosexual marriage is not stopped now, we will be having the exact same debate about "plural" marriages only one generation from now.

7

". . . And of Nature's God"

All of the arguments offered against homosexual marriage to this point have been entirely secular in nature. But it is legitimate to ask why, in this case, the movement to oppose homosexual marriage seems to be largely dominated by people who are deeply religious—specifically, by evangelical Protestants and conservative Roman Catholics. The answer is *not* that they are the only people with any *reason* to oppose homosexual marriage. It is, instead, that they (we) are the only people with the courage of our convictions on this issue.

While polls show that most Americans oppose homosexual marriage, they have been cowed into silence by a media and educational establishment that tell them homosexuality is normal and by judges who tell them it is a constitutional right. Only those who know that they answer to a higher authority have the courage to speak out against liberal opinion.

I do not want to end this book without making a very important point. *People of faith have every right to bring religiously informed convictions to bear on the making of public policy.* There is nothing—I repeat, nothing—in our Constitution, laws, or civic traditions that suggests that it is inappropriate for a citizen to do so.

Part of the problem is a grave misunderstanding of the concept of the "separation of church and state." My fellow Christians are sometimes fond of pointing out that the words "separation of church and state" never appear in the Constitution. This is true—the First Amendment prohibits only the "establishment" of religion, and protects "the free exercise thereof."

My approach is to acknowledge that the establishment and free exercise clauses imply a "separation of church and state," but then to clarify what this means. The founding fathers would have understood the "separation of church and state" as a separation of the institutions and offices of the church from the institutions and offices of the state. This means, for example, that the state cannot build and operate churches. Someone does not become bishop of a certain diocese by virtue of being elected to Congress. By the same token, one is not granted a seat in the Senate by virtue of leading a church denomination. Our head of state, the president, is not also the titular leader of a church, the way the Queen of England heads the Church of England. And participation in religious rituals, such as baptism or communion, cannot be mandated by the civil law. These are the types of intermingling of institutions and offices our system is designed to prevent.

The "separation of church and state," however, does not mean the separation of *God* and state, or the "establishment" of atheism, or the separation of faith and public policy. "Moral" arguments are *not* out of bounds in political debate. In fact, the supporters of homosexual marriage use moral arguments all the time when they use words like "justice" and "equality."

The efforts of political liberals to "keep religion out of politics" are entirely self-serving. They raised no objections when Christians led the movement to abolish slavery. They did not object in the 1950s when the Rev. Dr. Martin Luther King Jr. organized much of the civil rights movement in churches. They did not object in the 1960s, when liberal religious leaders opposed the Vietnam War on "moral" grounds. There was no liberal outcry about separating church and state in 1970s, when a born-again Christian who was also a liberal, Jimmy Carter, was elected president. In the 1980s, there was no liberal outcry when radical priests in Latin America promoted "liberation theology" or when liberal churches in the United States pushed for a nuclear freeze. And today, when religious groups cite the commandment "Thou shalt not kill" to oppose the death penalty, few liberals object. And today, what liberal objects when liberal Unitarian ministers argue in favor of "gay marriage?" It is simple hypocrisy, therefore, to say that Christians have no right to speak out *against* homosexual marriage.

Confirmation of this view has come from an unusual source. David Benkof wrote in the *San Francisco Chronicle*, "There are plenty of good civic reasons to defend the traditional definition of marriage." But he also insisted, "Religious teachings are sufficient cause to get involved in the political process and take a stand on a public issue." He even noted that:

> Historically, the left has opposed state-sponsored prayers in public institutions because they would unfairly stigmatize those who disagree with a given government-approved prayer. With *Goodridge*, the left now wants to put the government stamp on an institution that millions and millions of Americans can never make peace with because it goes against their deepest moral beliefs.[1]

What makes this notable? Benkof is an orthodox Jew. He was formerly a gay columnist and author under the name "David Bianco," until he announced that, for religious reasons, he was going to abstain from having sex with men.

A Christian View

Christianity supplied the moral foundations of the founding fathers and remains the dominant religion in America to this day. So it is important (and entirely appropriate) to highlight what Christianity brings to this public policy debate. What it brings most of all are first principles, because according to the Bible, marriage is an institution created by God.[2] Some liberal Christians, however, have been deceived into believing that Christianity itself does not require opposition to homosexuality or to homosexual marriage. So let me pause to explain why Christians should oppose homosexual marriage—if there was any doubt.

What is marriage for?[3]

1. Companionship

Psychologists say that human beings have a fundamental need for "stable primary bondings" with other people. In the Genesis account, God says, "It is not good for the man to be alone" (Genesis 2:18). In Genesis 2, Adam names the animals, but they are not "suitable" companions for him, because they are not the same as he—they are not human. To create a "suitable helper" for Adam, God creates woman. Adam and Eve will unite to become "one flesh" (Genesis 2:24).

Yet companionship alone does not define the purpose of marriage. The same Genesis passage that speaks of the man's need for companionship (Genesis 2:18–24) clearly shows God filling that need with another person who is like the man, yet different. She is someone who, by being of the opposite sex, serves to complement the man, not merely mirror him. Marriage unites opposites, each of whom has what the other lacks, and only in this way does it resolve the incompleteness that each feels when alone.

Furthermore, if one focuses exclusively on companionship as the purpose of marriage, it may lead to an excessively individualistic approach, geared only toward meeting the selfish desires of the individual. Yet marriage has a social function that goes beyond such limits.

2. Regulating sexual behavior

Marriage regulates sexual activity by channeling and containing it within specific boundaries. Throughout the Bible— from the Ten Commandments' proscription of adultery to

1 Corinthians 7:9—this is seen as one of marriage's legitimate and necessary functions. In fact, regulations to limit sexual behavior outside of marriage—whether by religious teachings, social taboos, or civil laws—are attempts to protect marriage because of its unique importance to society and even to protect the integrity of the individual as a creation of God (see, for instance, 1 Corinthians 6:12–20).

The importance to society might be obvious: Sex outside of marriage results in illegitimate children who will lack an intact family, while sex with multiple partners results in the spread of sexually transmitted diseases. Ironically, both of these problems have *increased*, not *decreased*, since the invention of the birth control pill and penicillin—technologies that were supposed to insulate us from these consequences.

The Bible sets definite sexual rules, and anthropologist Frank Beach has written, "There is not, and can never have been, a true society without sexual rules."[4] Yet the U.S. Supreme Court seems to have endorsed the nightmare vision of a society without sexual rules in its June 2003 decision striking down the Texas sodomy law.

3. Procreation and Child-Rearing

That reproduction of the human race is one of the central purposes of marriage is clear from God's mandate to Adam and Eve to "Be fruitful and increase in number; fill the earth and subdue it."[5] When Adam and Eve become "one flesh" they fulfill the purpose and meaning of marriage; their bodies are meant to complement one another; and their union is meant to produce children. Heterosexual couples who do not have children or who are incapable of having children still maintain the sexual complementarity. Homosexuals do not. This is not an arbitrary distinction, but a fundamental one. Homosexual couples are incapable of the natural purpose of marriage.

The Bible's teaching on homosexuality

The Bible's condemnation of homosexual acts is quite clear. There are at least eleven different passages, in both Testaments, which refer directly or indirectly to homosexuality, and all eleven either directly condemn homosexual practices as sinful or cast them in a clearly negative light.[6]

In the Old Testament, homosexuality is described as "detestable" (Leviticus 18:22). In the New Testament, the apostle Paul condemns the "shameful lusts," "indecent acts," and "perversion" involved in homosexuality (Romans 1:26–27). 1 Timothy 1:9–10 includes it in a list of very serious sins (several of which remain civil crimes to this day), comparing "homosexuals" to "those who kill their father or mothers,... murderers and immoral men...and kidnappers and liars and perjurers." The biblical case against homosexuality could not be more powerfully stated.

The Roman Catholic view

Although I, as an ordained Baptist minister, write from a Protestant perspective, the Roman Catholic teaching on this issue is essentially the same. A document released by the Vatican in 2003 pointed out that the Roman Catholic Church's opposition to homosexual marriage is grounded in natural law and is therefore applicable not only to believers, but "to all persons committed to promoting and defending the common good of society."[7]

Quoting the Catholic catechism, the statement declares that homosexual acts "do not proceed from a genuine affective and sexual complementarity. Under no circumstances can they be approved." As for the consequences, the document warns, "Allowing children to be adopted by persons living in such unions would actually mean doing violence to these children," because it would "place them in an environment that is not conducive to their full human development." As the statement makes clear, "Legal recognition of homosexual unions would obscure certain basic moral values and cause a devaluation of the institution of marriage."[8]

A brief note on religious liberty

Churches that support homosexual marriage already perform ceremonies to celebrate the "union" of homosexual couples, even in the forty-nine states where such unions are not legally recognized as marriage. If homosexual civil marriage spreads, religious liberty would demand that churches that oppose homosexual marriage and refuse to conduct such ceremonies be allowed to do so.

In other countries, the adoption of homosexual civil marriage has not led directly to punishing churches that refuse to "marry" same-sex couples. But the growing official affirmation of homosexuality (of which homosexual "marriage" is only one symptom) has led to "hate crime" laws that *have* been used to punish religious believers for even peacefully expressing their moral and religious opposition to homosexuality. For example, in the Canadian province of Saskatchewan, the Human Rights Commission actually fined both a newspaper and an advertiser for running an ad that quoted biblical verses condemning homosexuality.[9]

8

Where Do We Go from Here?

With President Bush's statement on February 24, 2004, announcing his support for an amendment to the U.S. Constitution to define marriage as the union of one man and one woman, the Federal Marriage Amendment has emerged as the best-known solution being offered to the problem of potential homosexual civil marriages. Yet, while a huge percentage of the American public believes marriage should be limited to the union of one man and one woman, the percentage that supports a Federal Marriage Amendment is somewhat smaller. Even among those who profess to believe that marriage should be between one man and one woman (whose number, incidentally, include most liberal Democratic politicians, such as former president Bill Clinton and senator and presidential candidate John Kerry), there is resistance to the idea of amending the U.S. Constitution.

But the Federal Marriage Amendment is now the only realistic option for protecting the historic definition of marriage. Liberal judicial activism has left us no choice.

Conservatives, as a rule, shy away from using the courts. Though a number of conservative groups did file lawsuits on the issue of gay marriage in 2004, it was to demand the enforcement of existing law against local officials who were breaking the law. It is the homosexual activists who have filed numerous suits around the country demanding that existing laws—and the will of the people—be overturned to suit them.[1]

The threat to traditional marriage is bound to grow. We've already seen this at the state level. In 2003 in California, the liberal legislature and Democratic governor Gray Davis—just shortly before he was recalled from office—passed a stealthily designed "domestic partnership" benefits bill (Assembly Bill 205) that amounts in effect to a "civil unions" bill. This was despite the fact that an open civil unions bill had been defeated the year before and even though California voters had previously enacted an initiative defining marriage as a union between one man and one woman. One of the political threats to traditional marriage lies in liberal legislatures performing such subterfuges.

But legislative actions can be undone by the people. By far the bigger problem is the courts, as we've seen with judicially ordered benefits (as in Vermont), judicially ordered homosexual civil marriage (as in Massachusetts), and judicially ordered recognition of out-of-state unions is already in litigation.

Conservatives who want to preserve existing law are still playing defense against an assault by homosexual activists. If homosexual activists really believe that they should have a "right" to homosexual marriage, then *they* should be the ones campaigning for a constitutional amendment to secure that right. But this is the one—in fact, the only—theoretical method of securing a "right" to homosexual marriage that is *not* being pursued by homosexual activists. The reason is clear—they know it would be impossible for them to get the approval of two-thirds of Congress and three-quarters of the states, as is necessary to amend the Constitution. But thanks to liberal activist judges, conservatives have been forced to consider amending the Constitution to enshrine the original intent of the marriage laws in all fifty states.

State-level fixes, with legislatively enacted Defense of Marriage Acts (DOMAs), are vulnerable. For instance, Indiana's DOMA declares straightforwardly, "Only a female may marry a male. Only a male may marry a female." It goes on to state, "A marriage between persons of the same gender is void in Indiana even if the marriage is lawful in the place where it is solemnized."[2] A simple DOMA of this type does not prevent a state from granting all of the legal rights and benefits of marriage to homosexual couples under a different name from "marriage," which is what happened in Vermont (which did not have a DOMA) at the behest of the courts. It also happened as a result of legislative action in California, even though that state did have a DOMA, adopted overwhelmingly by the voters in 2000, declaring, "Only marriage between a man and a woman is valid or recognized in California."[3]

The problem is that simple Defense of Marriage Acts are not a permanent fix, because they can either be repealed or sidestepped by a future legislature, or declared unconstitutional by either a state or a federal court. These vulnerabilities have led some states to propose "super-DOMAs" that preclude not only civil marriage, but the granting of marital benefits to homosexual couples, and that can be adopted as constitutional amendments, rather than merely as statutes. This would make them more difficult to repeal in the future, and would also make it impossible for a state court to overturn them on constitutional grounds.

Alaska did this by banning homosexual civil marriage in a constitutional amendment, which declares that "a marriage may exist only between one man and one woman."[4] At the same time, Alaska has a statutory provision declaring, "A same-sex relationship may not be recognized by the state as being entitled to the benefits of marriage."[5]

Nebraska is an example of a state that has adopted the strongest possible statewide DOMA, one which bans both homosexual marriage and marital benefits directly in the constitution, declaring:

> Only marriage between a man and a woman shall be valid or recognized in Nebraska. The uniting of two persons of the same sex in a civil union, domestic partnership, or other similar same-sex partnership shall not be valid or recognized in Nebraska.[6]

Yet even a strong DOMA like Nebraska's can be overruled in a moment by a federal court ruling ordering either recognition of interstate homosexual marriages or recognition of homosexual marriage across the board.

Because marriage law has historically been left to the states, that is where most of the action has been on defending marriage. In fact, at this writing, thirty-eight states have already adopted DOMAs in one form or another. Legislative proposals to add a DOMA have been introduced in every one of the remaining twelve states except for New Mexico. And in November 2004, five states that already have statutory DOMAs will have measures on the ballot to upgrade them to constitutional amendments.

The Federal Defense of Marriage Act

As we've seen, in 1996 Congress passed the federal Defense of Marriage Act by overwhelming bipartisan margins in both houses of Congress, and it was signed into law by President Bill Clinton.[7] The federal DOMA declared the right of states *not* to recognize "a relationship between persons of the same sex that is treated as a marriage" under the laws of another state. And it declared that for all purposes under *federal* law, "the word 'marriage' means only a legal union between one man and one woman as husband and wife."[8]

The federal Defense of Marriage Act has many gaps, however. It says nothing whatsoever about marital benefits that might be granted under some other name than civil "marriage." It would not, for instance, prevent the granting of marital benefits to same-sex partners under federal law, as long as the words "marriage" or "spouse" were not used. Legislation to grant employment benefits to the "domestic partners" of federal employees has already been introduced by homosexual Democratic congressman Barney Frank of Massachusetts.[9]

The federal DOMA also does not *prevent* states from recognizing homosexual marriages from other states, which could leave the decision in the hands of a liberal state attorney general. The federal DOMA has no impact on the decision of any state legislature to legalize homosexual marriage (a remote possibility in any state at this point), and it also does nothing to prevent a court from declaring that homosexual marriage must be allowed under the terms of a state constitution (as happened in Massachusetts in the *Goodridge* case).

Jurisdictional Limitation ("Court-Stripping")

Some argue that the best action Congress can take is to enact legislation to rein in the courts by limiting their jurisdiction over particular subjects. Congress has the right to do this at the federal level, because Article III, Section 2 of the U.S. Constitution gives appellate jurisdiction over most areas of law to the Supreme Court, but "with such exceptions, and under such regulations as the Congress shall make."

Republican congressman John Hostettler of Indiana has sought to limit the jurisdiction of the federal courts over marriage by introducing House Resolution 3313, the "Marriage Protection Act." This bill declares, "No court created by an Act of Congress shall have any jurisdiction, and the Supreme Court shall have no appellate jurisdiction, to hear or determine any question pertaining to the interpretation" of the federal Defense of Marriage Act.

This well-intentioned bill is worthy of support to send a message that Congress, not unelected judges, is the ultimate authority over public policy. But it would have no effect whatsoever on renegade judges at the state level, like those in Vermont and Massachusetts.

It is also far from certain that such a bill would be successful in achieving even its limited aims, even if it could be enacted. The notion of "judicial supremacy," while without foundation in the original intent of the authors of the Constitution, has nevertheless taken deep root in the minds of both public officials and the public at large. If the U.S. Supreme Court were to declare that the "Marriage Protection Act" itself is unconstitutional (because that same Article III, Section 2 says that "the judicial power shall extend to all cases . . . arising under this Constitution"), it is far from clear that any other governmental body would be willing to defy the Court.

Such an approach was tried, for instance, in Massachusetts, in an effort to nullify the effect of that state's Supreme Judicial Court ruling in the *Goodridge* case. In the Massachusetts state constitution, there is not just a vague legislative power to limit the jurisdiction of the courts. Instead, there is a specific provision declaring, "All causes of marriage, divorce, and alimony, and all appeals from judges of probate shall be heard and determined by the governor and council, until the legislature shall, by law, make other provision." Despite this clear statement that the governor, not the courts, has jurisdiction over marriage in Massachusetts, an appeal on these grounds was rejected (by the SJC, of course) and Republican governor Mitt Romney, although a strong opponent of the *Goodridge* decision, was unwilling to openly defy the court.

Given the reality of our out-of-control judicial system, it is clear that the only effective option to defend the definition of marriage is an amendment to the United States Constitution.

The Federal Marriage Amendment

Though marriage law is traditionally state law, the federal government has been involved in defining marriage before. In the nineteenth century, many settlers in the Utah territory practiced polygamy. Because Americans fervently opposed polygamy, it took seven attempts and forty-seven years (from 1849 to 1896) for Utah to gain statehood. During that time, Congress passed three separate laws (which were upheld by the U.S. Supreme Court[10]) to outlaw and punish polygamy, and the Enabling Act that finally allowed Utah statehood provided explicitly that "polygamous or plural marriages are forever prohibited."[11] Utah complied, incorporating that precise language into its state constitution in a provision that is "irrevocable without the consent of the United States and the people of this State."[12] So there is a significant historical precedent for federal action to protect the fundamental definition of marriage.

The Federal Marriage Amendment that Congress is currently considering states:

> Marriage in the United States shall consist only of the union of a man and a woman. Neither this Constitution, nor the constitution of any State, shall be construed to require that marriage or the legal incidents thereof be conferred upon any union other than the union of a man and a woman.

The Federal Marriage Amendment would require all levels of government to define marriage as the union of one man and one woman. No state legislature, local official, or state or federal judge would be able to redefine marriage, as the Supreme Judicial Court of Massachusetts did on November 18, 2003. In addition, no court would be able to order that the legal *benefits* of marriage be granted to homosexual couples under some other name, such as civil unions or domestic partnerships, as the Vermont Supreme Court did in 2000. The Federal Marriage Amendment does leave open the possibility of state legislatures enacting civil unions, but such legislation would be open to public debate and political change, which is far better than having arbitrary binding decisions handed down by the courts.

What's at Stake

Marriage is the foundation of the family, and the family is the foundation of our society. The health and protection of marriage and the family is far more crucial to the future of our country than the timing of congressional pay raises—the subject of our most recently ratified Constitutional amendment.

Events in the courts have already made it clear that the Constitution *will*, de facto, be amended. It will either be amended by arrogant judges who write into that document "rights" that the founding fathers could never have conceived of, or it will be amended through the democratic process to protect our most fundamental institution.

Two questions are at stake here. Will we protect the institution of marriage? And will we protect the practice of democracy?

The answers are up to you.

ACKNOWLEDGMENTS

———

I want to thank Harry Crocker and John Lalor of Regnery Publishing for their interest in this book. I thank Bob Maginnis and Ken Connor, who brought me to the Family Research Council, and Alan Crippen, Colin Stewart, and Tony Perkins, who have supervised my work there. I am indebted to my talented colleagues Bridget Maher and Tim Dailey for their work.

Most of all, I thank my wife and son for tolerating the time that I took away from them to write this book.

Peter Sprigg
Washington, D.C.
May 19, 2004

NOTES

Chapter One: Who Declared This Culture War? How We Got Here

1. Doug Ireland, "Republicans Relaunch the Antigay Culture Wars," *The Nation*, October 20, 2003.

2. John Sonego, "The antigay industry wants you!" *The Advocate*, October 10, 2003.

3. Bruce Carroll, "A fine mess we're in now," *Washington Blade*, April 23, 2004.

4. Robin Cheryl Miller, "Marriage Between Persons of Same Sex," 81 *American Law Reports* 5th 1, September 2002.

5. *Lawrence et al. v. Texas*, 123 S. Ct. 2472 (2003): 6, 17–18. Page numbers cited are from the respective opinions as published in the initial Bench Opinion.

6. Lino A. Graglia, "Single-Sex 'Marriage': The Role of the Courts," *Brigham Young University Law Review*, 2001.

Chapter Two: Why Libertarians (and Other People Who Might Surprise You) Should Support the Federal Marriage Amendment

1.   Elizabeth Mehren, "Acceptance of Gays Rises Among New Generation," *Los Angeles Times*, April 11, 2004.

2.   Adoption of the amendment cannot be completed until November 2006.

3.   In doing so, the court explicitly reversed the precedent it had set only seventeen years earlier in the case of *Bowers v. Hardwick*, in which a Georgia sodomy law had been upheld. Of the six justices who voted to strike down the Texas law in 2003, only Sandra Day O'Connor based her judgment on "equal protection" grounds—the fact that the Texas law, unlike the earlier Georgia one, punished only homosexual conduct, not the same sexual acts when committed by heterosexuals. The other five justices (still an absolute majority of the Court) relied on the more expansive "privacy" argument, thus effectively striking down all sodomy laws, even those that were neutral with respect to the sex of the participants. Under this ruling, no homosexual civilian in the United States will ever again be subject to criminal prosecution in any state merely for engaging in private, consensual homosexual acts with another adult. The "homosexual privacy" battle has already been fought, and the homosexuals have already won, though at least two of the assumptions that were at least implicit in the court's ruling are extremely dubious. The first is the assumption that moral values are an inherently illegitimate basis for making laws, especially criminal laws. The sec-

ond is the assumption that apart from whatever moral offense it might cause to certain individuals, homosexual acts are not intrinsically harmful to any individuals or to society as a whole. This is demonstrably false, and can be shown to be false based on the medical and public health consequences of homosexual acts alone, entirely without reference to any moral code. One of the gravest errors made by the state of Texas in its defense before the Supreme Court was its failure to effectively argue the public health issue.

4.   These amendments undid the infamous "three-fifths" compromise in the original U.S. Constitution, which is often oversimplified as having declared that black slaves were only "three-fifths of a person." I call this an oversimplification because many people forget that it was the slave-owning South that wanted slaves counted as full persons for the purpose of increasing their representation in the U.S. House of Representatives, while it was the anti-slavery North that did not want slaves counted at all, as long as they were not granted the rights of citizenship. The decision to count three-fifths of slaves was a purely political compromise over the relative political power of the states in Congress, and had nothing to do with a conscious calculation of the human value of those slaves as individuals.

5.   Cited in Maggie Gallagher, "Are you a bigot?" Townhall.com, March 3, 2004.

6.   Raphael Lewis, "Foes of gay marriage try long shot," *Boston Globe*, April 20, 2004. I would be remiss if I did not

note the heroic efforts in defense of marriage in the Massachusetts legislature by Representative Philip Travis of Rehoboth, who was the principal sponsor of the original Marriage Affirmation and Protection Amendment ("MA&PA"), and of Representative Emile Goguen of Fitchburg, who has directly challenged the legitimacy of the Supreme Judicial Court's decision by introducing a "bill of address" to remove the four offending justices from office. Both are Democrats (and the latter was an acquaintance of the author in my own days as a liberal Democratic activist in Fitchburg in the late 1970s and early 1980s).

7.   Ibid.

8.   It is a myth that homosexuals are "born gay" so it is not far-fetched that more men might adopt the homosexual lifestyle by choice. On the myth of "born gay," see Chapter Three.

9.   "About 1.4 percent of the women said they thought of themselves as homosexual or bisexual and about 2.8 percent of the men identified themselves in this way." Robert T. Michael, John H. Gagnon, Edward O. Laumann, and Gina Kolata, *Sex in America: A Definitive Survey* (Boston: Little, Brown and Co., 1994), 176–77.

10.   Maggie Gallagher, "The message of same-sex marriage," Townhall.com, January 8, 2004.

11.   Men lose in other ways too, as has been documented by, among others, George Gilder in his book *Men and Marriage* (Gretna, LA: Pelican, 1992).

12.   For examples, see Chapter Five.

13. A copy of these remarks is available online. See Paul Nathanson and Katherine K. Young, "Marriage-a-la-mode: Answering the Advocates of Gay Marriage," at http://www.marriageinstitute.ca/pages/Young%20and%20 Nathanson1.htm.

Chapter Three: Is Rosie O'Donnell the New Rosa Parks? The Civil Rights Arguments

1. Cheryl Wetzstein, "Blacks angered by gays' metaphors," *Washington Times*, March 2, 2004.
2 *The American Heritage Dictionary*, s.v. "civil rights."
3. Civil Rights Act of 1964, PL 88-352.
4. Edward Stein, *The Mismeasure of Desire* (New York: Oxford University Press, 1999), 138.
5. Simon LeVay, "A Difference in Hypothalmic Structure Between Heterosexual and Homosexual Men," *Science* 253, August 1991.
6. Stein, 197.
7. LeVay, 1035–36.
8. William Byne and Bruce Parsons, "Human Sexual Orientation: The Biologic Theories Appraised," *Archives of General Psychiatry* 50, March 1993.
9. J. Michael Bailey and Richard C. Pillard, "A Genetic Study of Male Sexual Orientation," *Archives of General Psychiatry* 48, December 1991.
10. Scott L. Hershberger, "A Twin Registry Study of Male and Female Sexual Orientation," *The Journal of Sex Research* 34. no. 2, 1997.

11. Byne and Parsons, 235.

12. Dean H. Hamer, Stella Hu, Victoria L. Magnuson, Nan Hu, Angela M. L. Pattatucci, "A Linkage Between DNA Markers on the X Chromosome and Male Sexual Orientation," *Science* 261, July 1993.

13. Ibid.

14. Ibid.

15. Ibid.

16. Ibid.

17. George Rice, Carol Anderson, Neil Risch, and George Ebers, "Male Homosexuality: Absence of Linkage to Microsatellite Markers at Xq28," *Science* 284, April 1999.

18. Ibid.

19. Byne and Parsons, 228.

20. Robert T. Michael, John H. Gagnon, Edward O. Laumann, and Gina Kolata, *Sex in America: A Definitive Survey* (Boston: Little, Brown and Co., 1994), 176–77.

21. Edward O. Laumann, John H. Gagnon, Robert T. Michael, and Stuart Michaels, *The Social Organization of Sexuality: Sexual Practices in the United States* (Chicago: The University of Chicago Press, 1994), 311–12.

22. Robert L. Spitzer, M.D., "Can Some Gay Men and Lesbians Change Their Sexual Orientation? 200 Participants Reporting a Change from Homosexual to Heterosexual Orientation," *Archives of Sexual Behavior* 32, no. 5, October 2003.

23. Ibid.

24. R. Goetze, *Homosexuality and the possibility of change: An ongoing research project.* Cited in Spitzer. http://www.newdirection.ca/research/ index.html.

25. "The Ties That Divide: A Conversation on Gay Marriage with Andrew Sullivan and Gerard Bradley," Washington, D.C.: The Pew Forum on Religion & Public Life, April 28, 2004.

26. A. P. Bell and M. S. Weinberg, *Homosexualities: A Study of Diversity Among Men and Women* (New York: Simon and Schuster, 1978), 308, 309. See also A. P. Bell, M. S. Weinberg, and S. K. Hammersmith, *Sexual Preference* (Bloomington: Indiana University Press, 1981).

27. Paul Van de Ven et al., "A Comparative Demographic and Sexual Profile of Older Homosexually Active Men," *Journal of Sex Research* 34, 1997.

28. Katherine Fethers et al., "Sexually Transmitted Infections and Risk Behaviors in Women Who have Sex with Women," *Sexually Transmitted Infections* 76, 2000.

29. Centers for Disease Control and Prevention, *HIV/AIDS Surveillance Report*, 2001; Vol. 13, No. 2.

30. Laumann et al., 298.

31. Vincent M. B. Silenzio, M.D., "Ten Things Gay Men Should Discuss with their Health Care Providers: Commentary," http://www.glma.org/news/releases/n02071710 gaythings.html.

32. Fethers et al., "Sexually Transmitted Infections and Risk Behaviors in Women Who have Sex with Women."

33. D. Fergusson et al., "Is Sexual Orientation Related to Mental Health Problems and Suicidality in Young People?" *Archives of General Psychiatry* 56, October 1999.

34. Silenzio, "Ten Things Gay Men Should Discuss with their Health Care Providers."

35. Katherine A. O'Hanlan, M.D., "Ten Things Lesbians Should Discuss with their Health Care Providers: Commentary," http://www.glma.org/news/releases/n02071710 lesbianthings.html.

36. Lettie L. Lockhart et al., "Letting out the Secret: Violence in Lesbian Relationships," *Journal of Interpersonal Violence* 9, 1994.

37. David Island and Patrick Letellier, *Men Who Beat the Men Who Love Them: Battered Gay Men and Domestic Violence* (New York: Haworth Press, 1991).

38. Kurt Freund et al., "Pedophilia and Heterosexuality vs. Homosexuality," *Journal of Sex & Marital Therapy* 10, 1984.

39. Kurt Freund, Robin Watson, and Douglas Rienzo, "Heterosexuality, Homosexuality, and Erotic Age Preference," *The Journal of Sex Research* 26, No. 1, February 1989.

40. W. D. Erickson, "Behavior Patterns of Child Molesters," *Archives of Sexual Behavior* 17, 1988.

41. Cited in Michael P. Farris, Jordan W. Lorence, Joshua W. Carden, Brief *Amicus Curiae* of the Center for the Original Intent of the Constitution in Support of Respondent, *John Geddes Lawrence and Tyron Garner v. The State of Texas*, Supreme Court of the United States, No. 02-102, February 18, 2003.

42. "King's widow gives her support to gay marriage, controversial among civil rights leaders," Associated Press, March 24, 2004.

43. John Lewis, "At a Crossroads on Gay Unions," *Boston Globe*, October 25, 2003.

44. Lou Chibbaro, Jr., "Edwards slams Dean for dodging 'guns, God and gays'," *Washington Blade*, December 26, 2003.

45. "Day to Day," National Public Radio, February 12, 2004.

46. Jay Lindsay, "Blacks Object to Gay Marriage Comparison," Associated Press, November 28, 2003.

47. Herbert A. Sample, "For many blacks, gay fight isn't theirs," *Sacramento Bee*, March 16, 2004.

48. Doug Ireland, "Republicans Relaunch the Antigay Culture Wars," *The Nation*, October 20, 2003.

49. "The Nation's reportedly 'gay' columnist draws fire," news release, American Family Association of Michigan, October 9, 2003.

50. "Black Pastors Rally Against Gay Marriage," Associated Press, March 23, 2004.

51. Lindsay, "Blacks Object to Gay Marriage Comparison."

52. Sample, "For many blacks, gay fight isn't theirs."

53. George E. Curry, "Mixed Feelings About Same Sex Marriages," December 8, 2002. www.georgecurry.com.

54. Phuong Ly and Hamil R. Harris, "Blacks, Gays in Struggle of Values; Same-Sex Marriage Issue Challenges Religious, Political Ties," *Washington Post*, March 15, 2004.

55. Star Parker, "Gay Politics, Black Reality," Townhall.com, January 12, 2004.

56. This account is drawn from Matthew J. Franck, "Not *Loving* It," *National Review Online*, March 16, 2004, and Derrick Z. Jackson, "Echoes of racism in gay marriage ban," *Boston Globe*, April 2, 2004.

57. *Loving v. Virginia*, 388 U.S., 12.

58. *Perez v. Sharp*, 32 Cal.2d 717 (1948).

59. *Loving v. Virginia*, 388 U.S., 12.

60. *Ruth Morrison, et al. v. Doris Anne Sadler, et al.* Marion County Superior Court, Indiana, Cause No. 49D13-0211-PL-001946, May 7, 2003.

61. *Mark Lewis and Dennis Winslow, et al. v. Gwendolyn L. Harris*, Superior Court of New Jersey, Mercer County, Docket No.: MER-L-15-03, November 5, 2003, 50-53.

Chapter Four: "The Laws of Nature" and the Public Purpose of Marriage

1. For a more extensive discussion, see Maggie Gallagher, "What is Marriage For? The Public Purposes of Marriage Law," *Louisiana Law Review* 62, No. 3, Spring 2002.

2. Nadine F. Marks and James David Lambert, "Marital Status Continuity and Change Among Young and Midlife Adults," *Journal of Family Issues* 19, November 1998.

3. Catherine E. Ross et al., "The Impact of the Family on Health: The Decade in Review," *Journal of Marriage and the Family* 52, November 1990.

4. Bureau of Justice Statistics, *Intimate Partner Violence*, National Crime Victimization Survey, U.S. Department of Justice, Washington, D.C., May 2000.

5. Bureau of Justice Statistics, *Criminal Victimization 1999: Changes 1998–1999 with Trends 1993–1999*, National Crime Victimization Survey, U.S. Department of Justice, Washington, D.C., August 2000.

6. Linda J. Waite, ed., *The Ties That Bind: Perspectives on Marriage and Cohabitation* (New York: Aldine de Gruyter, 2000), 385–86.

7.   Edward O. Laumann et al., *The Social Organization of Sexuality: Sexual Practices in the United States* (Chicago: University of Chicago Press, 1994), 364.

8.   Kristin A. Moore, "Nonmarital School-Age Motherhood: Family, Individual, and School Characteristics," *Journal of Adolescent Research* 13, October 1998.

9.   John P. Hoffman and Robert A. Johnson, "A National Portrait of Family Structure and Adolescent Drug Use," *Journal of Marriage and the Family* 60, August 1998.

10. Chris Coughlin and Samuel Vucinich, "Family Experience in Preadolescence and the Development of Male Delinquency," *Journal of Marriage and the Family* 58, May 1996.

11. Deborah A. Dawson, "Family Structure and Children's Health and Well-Being: Data from the 1988 National Health Interview Survey on Child Health," *Journal of Marriage and the Family* 53, August 1991.

12. Federal Interagency Forum on Child and Family Statistics, *America's Children: Key Indicators of Well-Being 2001*, Washington, D.C.

13. Dawson, "Family Structure and Children's Health and Well-Being: Data from the 1988 National Health Interview Survey on Child Health."

14. Paul R. Amato and Alan Booth, *A Generation at Risk: Growing Up in an Era of Family Upheaval* (Cambridge, MA: Harvard University Press, 1997), 111–15.

15. Adam Goldman, "Oops—Britney Spears marriage annulled," Associated Press, January 6, 2004.

16. Lance Gay, "In 1906, Teddy Urged Marriage Amendment," *Commercial Appeal* (Memphis, TN), March 7, 2004.

Chapter Five: Same-Sex Marriage:
Who Needs It? Who Wants It?

1. U.S. General Accounting Office, *Defense of Marriage Act*, GAO-04-353R.

2. *Hillary Goodridge et al. vs. Department of Public Health*, SJC-08860 (Mass.), November 18, 2003.

3. Lambda Legal Defense and Education Fund, *Life Planning: Legal Documents and Protections for Lesbians and Gay Men* (New York: Lambda Legal Defense and Education Fund, 1998). http://www.lambdalegal.org/sections/library/life-planning.pdf.

4. Human Rights Campaign, *Legal Documents to Protect Your Family*, www.hrc.org.

5. There is no evidence that homosexuals are routinely denied the right to visit their partners in the hospital. When this issue was raised in 1996 during debate over the Defense of Marriage Act, the Family Research Council did an informal survey of nine hospitals in four states and the District of Columbia. None of the administrators surveyed could recall a single case in which a visitor was barred because of his or her homosexuality, and they were incredulous that this would even be considered an issue. Family Research Council, "Hospital Visitation: A Non-Issue," *InFocus*, 1996.

6. Lambda Legal Defense and Education Fund, 3.

7. http://216.36.240.148/Advance/documents_set.html

8. Human Rights Campaign, *The Costs of Estate Planning*, online at www.hrc.org.

9. My thanks to Allan C. Carlson for much of this explana-
    tion of the history of Social Security. Any errors, however,
    are those of the author.

10. www.10percent.com.

11. http://tps.studentorg.wisc.edu/.

12. www.tenpercentbent.com/.

13. www.broadwayplaypubl.com/tenp.htm.

14. *http://www.glsen.org/cgibin/iowa/educator/booklink/record/*
    1525.html, http://www.epfl.net/booklists/booklist2.cfm?LIST
    _ID=33

15. Human Rights Campaign, National Gay & Lesbian Task
    Force, Parents, Families & Friends of Lesbians & Gays,
    National Center for Lesbian Rights, Gay & Lesbian Advo-
    cates & Defenders, Gay & Lesbian Alliance Against
    Defamation, Pride At Work AFL-CIO, People For the
    American Way Foundation, Anti-Defamation League,
    Mexican American Legal Defense & Education Fund,
    Puerto Rican Legal Defense & Education Fund, Society of
    American Law Teachers, Soulforce, Stonewall Law Associ-
    ation of Greater Houston, Equality Alabama, Equality
    Florida, S.A.V.E., Community Center of Idaho, Your Fam-
    ily, Friends & Neighbors, Kansas Unity & Pride Alliance,
    Louisiana Electorate of Gays & Lesbians, Equality Missis-
    sippi, Promo, North Carolina Gay & Lesbian Attorneys,
    Cimarron Foundation of Pride Movement, Alliance for
    Full Acceptance, Gay & Lesbian Community Center of
    Utah, and Equality Virginia. Brief *Amicus Curiae* in sup-
    port of petitioners. *Lawrence and Garner v. State of Texas*,
    No. 02-102. U.S. March 26, 2003.

16. Ibid.

17. Ibid.

18. "American Fact Finder." United States Census Bureau, http://factfinder.census.gov/servlet/QTTable?ds_name=DEC_2000_SF1_U&geo_id=01000US&qr_name=DEC_2000_SF1_U_DP1.

19. Ibid.

20. Edward O. Laumann, John H. Gagnon, Robert T. Michael, and Stuart Michaels, *The Social Organization of Sexuality: Sexual Practices in the United States* (Chicago: University of Chicago Press, 1994), Table 8.3B, 311.

21. Ibid., Table 8.3A, 311.

22. Ibid., 287.

23. Ibid., 288.

24. Ibid., 289.

25. Ibid., 289, footnote 7; citing Bruce Voeller, "Some uses and abuses of the Kinsey scale," in *Homosexuality-Heterosexuality: Concepts of Sexual Orientation*, ed. David P. McWhirter, Stephanie A. Saunders, and June Machover Reinisch (New York: Oxford University Press, 1990).

26. Tavia Simmons and Martin O'Connell, "Married-Couple and Unmarried-Partner Households: 2000," Census 2000 Special Reports, 4, Table 2. http://www.census.gov/prod/2003pubs/censr-5.pdf.

27. Ibid.

28. The 2000 census reports 4,849,033 persons eighteen years of age and over in Massachusetts. DP-1. Profile of General Demographic Characteristics: 2000 (Massachusetts). http://factfinder.census.gov/servlet/BasicFactsTable?_lang=en&_vt_name=DEC_2000_SF1_U_DP1&_geo_id=04000US25.

29. Fred Bayles, "Vermont's gay civil unions mostly affairs of the heart: Law didn't spur legal battles or an 'invasion'," *USA Today* (January 7, 2004).

30. Simmons and O'Connell, "Married-Couple and Unmarried-Partner Households: 2000."

31. All of the foregoing poll data is drawn from: "Attitudes About Homosexuality & Gay Marriage," AEI Studies in Public Opinion, American Enterprise Institute, April 23, 2004. http://www.aei.org/publications/pubID.14882, filter.social/pub_detail.asp

32. The Polling Company, "Same-Sex Marriage, Civil Unions and Federal Marriage Amendment: Key Findings," April 7, 2004. http://www.pollingcompany.com/news.asp

33. James T. Sears, "Marriage license or just license?" *Washington Blade*, August 22, 2003.

34. Suzanna Walters, "Gays right to marry?" *Baltimore Sun*, September 30, 2003.

35. Paul Flynn, "White Wedding? No, Thanks," *The Guardian*, October 11, 2003, and *Guardian Weekend*.

36. Clifford Krauss, "Now Free to Marry, Canada's Gays Say, 'Do I?'" *New York Times*, August 31, 2001.

37. Quoted in Michael Foust, "Homosexuals oppose same-sex 'marriage,' magazine poll suggests," *BP News* (Baptist Press), April 7, 2004.

38. Mubarak Dahir, "Nattering nabobs among our own," *Washington Blade*, March 5, 2004.

39. Andrew Sullivan, "Why The M Word Matters To Me," *Time*, February 16, 2004.

Chapter Six: What Harm Would It Do?

1. Nicholas Wapshott, "The private face of the bishop-elect," *Ottawa Citizen*, August 5, 2003, and Dave Munday, "Episcopalians Vote in Favor of Gay Bishop," *Post and Courier* (Charleston, S.C.), August 4, 2003.

2. Gene Robinson, interviewed by Terry Gross, "Fresh Air," National Public Radio, July 24, 2003.

3. Jasper Gerard, "I want to be a good bishop not a gay bishop," *Sunday Times* (London), August 10, 2003.

4. Judith Stacey and Timothy J. Biblarz, "(How) Does the Sexual Orientation of Parents Matter," *American Sociological Review* 66, 2001.

5. Paul A. Nakonezny and Robert D. Shull, "The Effect of No-Fault Divorce Law on the Divorce Rate Across the 50 States and Its Relation to Income, Education, and Religiosity," *Journal of Marriage and the Family* 57, May 1995.

6. Maggie Gallagher, *The Abolition of Marriage: How We Destroy Lasting Love* (Washington, D.C.: Regnery, 1996), 150.

7. Stanley Kurtz, "The End of Marriage in Scandinavia: The 'conservative case' for same-sex marriage collapses," *Weekly Standard*, February 2, 2004.

8. Maria Xiridou, et al, "The Contribution of Steady and Casual Partnerships to the Incidence of HIV Infection among Homosexual Men in Amsterdam," *AIDS* 17, 2003.

9. Edward O. Laumann et al., *The Social Organization of Sexuality: Sexual Practices in the United States* (Chicago: University of Chicago Press, 1994), 216.

10. National Center for Health Statistics, Centers for Disease Control, 43 Percent of First Marriages Break Up Within 15 Years. http://www.cdc.gov/nchs/releases/01news/first-marr.htm.

11. David P. McWhirter and Andrew M. Mattison, *The Male Couple: How Relationships Develop* (Englewood Cliffs: Prentice-Hall, 1984), 252, 253.

12. Gunnar Andersson, Turid Noack, Ane Seiestad, and Harald Weedon-Fekjaer, "Divorce-Risk Patterns in Same-Sex 'Marriages' in Norway and Sweden," paper presented at the 2004 Annual Meeting of the Population Association of America, April 3, 2004. http://paa2004.princton.edu/download.asp?submissionId=40208.

13. Kyle D. Pruett, *Fatherneed: Why Father Care Is as Essential as Mother Care for Your Child* (New York: The Free Press, 2000).

14. Brenda Hunter, *The Power of Mother Love: Transforming Both Mother and Child* (Colorado Springs, CO: Waterbrook Press, 1997).

15. Human Rights Campaign, Donor Agreement. http://www.hrc.org/Template.cfm?Section=Search_the_Law_Datbase& Template=/ContentManagement/ContentDisplay.cfm&ContentID=18669

16. Kurt Freund, Robin Watson, and Douglas Rienzo, "Heterosexuality, Homosexuality, and Erotic Age Preference," *Journal of Sex Research* 26, No. 1, February 1989.

17. W. D. Erickson, "Behavior Patterns of Child Molesters," *Archives of Sexual Behavior* 17, 1988. Although most child sexual abuse (whether homosexual or heterosexual) is

committed by men, lesbian sexual abuse has also been reported. For example, in the middle of the debate over a marriage amendment in Massachusetts, the *Boston Herald* reported, "A lesbian foster parent allegedly raped a 15-year-old girl in her custody twice last month. Department of Social Services officials said [Christina] Machado had a near-spotless record in eight years as a foster parent." See David R. Guarino, "Rape rap fuels gay fight: Lesbian foster mom charged in assault," *Boston Herald*, April 2, 2004.

18. Robert Lerner and Althea K. Nagai, *No Basis: What the Studies Don't Tell Us About Same Sex Parenting* (Washington: Ethics and Public Policy Center, 2001).

19. Stacey and Biblarz, "(How) Does the Sexual Orientation of Parents Matter."

20. Sotirios Sarantakos, "Children in three contexts: Family, education and social development," *Children Australia* 21, No. 3, 1996.

21. Kyneret Hope, "Of Lesbian Descent," in Louise Rafkin, editor, *Different Mothers: Sons and Daughters of Lesbians Talk About Their Lives* (Pittsburgh: Cleis Press, 1990), 59.

22. Ibid., "Out of the Pain," 110–16.

23. Ibid., Kathlean Hill, "Change and Consistency," 150.

24. Ibid., Carey Conley, "Always Changes," 157–59.

25. Jakii Edwards with Nancy Kurrack, *Like Mother, Like Daughter? The effects of growing up in a homosexual home* (Vienna, VA: Xulon Press, 2001), 8.

26. "Sen. Santorum's Comments on Homosexuality," Associated Press, April 22, 2003.

27. Human Rights Campaign, "National and Pennsylvania GLBT Civil Rights Groups Outraged at Santorum's 'Deeply Discriminatory' Remarks," April 21, 2003.

28. Ellen Goodman, "The Republican Theocracy," *Boston Globe*, May 1, 2003.

29. Jeffrey St. Clair, "Santorum: That's Latin for A**hole," [edited]; *Counterpunch*, May 1, 2003. www.counterpunch.org/stclair05012003.html.

30. Maureen Dowd, "Chest Banging, Here and There," *New York Times*, April 23, 2003.

31. Fordham University, Bronx, New York, December 3, 2003.

32. Kamil Zaheer, "Young Man Marries Own Grandmother," Reuters, March 19, 2004.

33. "Woman married dead boyfriend," Associated Press, February 11, 2004.

34. Richard Leiby with Anne Schroeder, "The Reliable Source: Annals of Puffery," *Washington Post*, March 21, 2004.

35. Richard Pyle, "Los Angeles Times Wins Five Pulitzers," Associated Press, April 6, 2004.

36. Don Lattin, "Committed to marriage for the masses: Polyamorists say they relate honestly to multiple partners," *San Francisco Chronicle*, April 20, 2004.

37. Joe Crea, "Polygamy advocates buoyed by gay court wins: Some see sodomy, marriage opinions as helping their cause," *Washington Blade*, December 26, 2003.

38. Alexandria Sage, "Attorney challenges Utah ban on polygamy, cites Texas sodomy case," Associated Press, January 12, 2004.

Chapter Seven: "...And of Nature's God"

1. David Benkof, "Religious views have a place in same-sex marriage debate," *San Francisco Chronicle*, January 18, 2004.

2. See Genesis 2:18–24.

3. I am indebted for much of this discussion to Stanley J. Grenz, *Sexual Ethics: An Evangelical Perspective* (Lousiville, KY: Westminster John Knox Press, 1990).

4. Frank A. Beach, ed., *Human Sexuality in Four Perspectives* (Baltimore: Johns Hopkins University Press, 1977), 116.

5. Genesis 1:28.

6. Genesis 13:13, Genesis 19:1–11 (especially verses 4–7), Leviticus 18:6–30 (especially verse 22), Leviticus 20:10–24 (especially verse 13), Deuteronomy 23:17–18, Judges 19:22–25 (especially verses 22–23), Job 36:13–14 (especially verse 14), Romans 1:18–32 (especially verses 26–27), 1 Corinthians 6:9–20 (especially verses 9–10), 1 Timothy 1:8–11 (especially verse 10), Jude 4–19 (especially verse 7). A key verse in the Old Testament is Leviticus 18:22: "Do not lie with a man as one lies with a woman; that is detestable." Advocates of homosexuality are fond of dismissing this by pointing to other passages of Leviticus featuring ritual prohibitions that are no longer considered binding. It's true that looking at the context is an important principle of biblical interpretation. But the immediate context of this verse in Leviticus is telling. The verse immediately before it condemns child sacrifice, and the verse immediately after it condemns bestiality. Are we to discard the moral guidance of those verses as well? The

passage in Romans is also a crucial one, because it makes clear that homosexuality is not just a violation of some ritual law, but is contrary to God's entire created order in nature. It begins by saying: "The wrath of God is being revealed from heaven against all the godlessness and wickedness of men who suppress the truth by their wickedness." It goes on to say, "Because of this, God gave them over to shameful lusts. Even their women exchanged natural relations for unnatural ones. In the same way the men also abandoned natural relations with women and were inflamed with lust for one another. Men committed indecent acts with other men, and received in themselves the due penalty for their perversion." 1 Timothy 1:9–10 includes homosexuality in a list of very serious sins (several of which remain civil crimes to this day): " . . . law is not made for a righteous person, but for those who are lawless and rebellious, for the ungodly and sinners, for the unholy and profane, for those who kill their fathers or mothers, for murderers and immoral men and homosexuals and kidnappers and liars and perjurers, and whatever else is contrary to sound teaching. . . ." Revisionist theologians have attempted to explain these straightforward passages away, but their interpretations have been convincingly refuted. For a comprehensive theological treatment, see Robert A. J. Gagnon, *The Bible and Homosexual Practice* (Nashville: Abingdon Press, 2001). For a more concise treatment, I recommend the Family Research Council publication by Timothy J. Dailey, *Keeping the Churches Marriage-Friendly: How Scripture and Tradition*

Refute the "Gay Theology" (Washington, DC: Family Research Council, 2001); available at 1-800-225-4008 or online at www.frc.org.

7. Congregation for the Doctrine of the Faith, *Considerations Regarding Proposals to Give Legal Recognition to Unions between Homosexual Persons* (Rome: Congregation for the Doctrine of the Faith), June 3, 2003.

8. Ibid.

9. Alan Sears and Craig Osten, *The Homosexual Agenda: Exposing the Principal Threat to Religious Freedom Today* (Nashville: Broadman & Holman, 2003), 182–83.

Chapter Eight: Where Do We Go from Here?

1. I am aware of only one suit that has ever been filed to overturn a legislatively enacted provision giving marital benefits (no legislative body in the country has ever granted full civil marriage) to homosexual couples. In Pennsylvania, conservative activists filed suit in state court against a Philadelphia law granting domestic partner benefits to homosexual couples, and won a lower court ruling that the Philadelphia provision violated state law because it amounted to a redefinition of marriage. Even this case, however, represents a jurisdictional dispute over whether a local government body has the right to change the definition of marriage, which is a state and not a local function. So it, too, represents an attempt to enforce current law, rather than an attempt to create new law.

2. Indiana Code Sec. 31-11-1-1.

3. Ca. Fam. Sec. 308.5.

4. Alaska Constitution, Article 1, Sec. 25.

5. Alaska Stat. 25.05.013 (b).

6. Neb. Const. Art. 1, Sec. 29.

7. Public Law 104-199, September 21, 1996.

8. Ibid.

9. H.R. 2426, introduced June 11, 2003—the day after homosexual marriage became legal in the Canadian province of Ontario.

10. See *Reynolds v. U. S.*, 98 U.S. 145 (1878).

11. Amy Ripperger, "Polygamy: The Political Precedence for Defining Marriage" (Witherspoon Fellowship project, Family Research Council, Spring 2004); see also Linda Thatcher, "A Chronology of Utah's Struggle for Statehood," http://historytogo.utah.gov/strugglechrono.html

12. Utah Constitution, Article III.

INDEX